W9-ADD-349

CASE STUDIES IN

CULTURAL ANTHROPOLOGY

GENERAL EDITORS
George and Louise Spindler
STANFORD UNIVERSITY

THE BARABAIG
East African Cattle-Herders

Map of Tanzania

 Political boundary

Roads (Main connecting)

• Towns and cities

Barabaig territory

DT 443
K55

THE BARABAIG
East African Cattle-Herders

By
GEORGE J. KLIMA
State University of New York at Albany

HOLT, RINEHART AND WINSTON
NEW YORK   CHICAGO   SAN FRANCISCO   ATLANTA
DALLAS   MONTREAL   TORONTO   LONDON   SYDNEY

188879

Copyright © 1970 by Holt, Rinehart and Winston, Inc.
All rights reserved
Library of Congress Catalog Card Number: 74-100385
ISBN: 0-03-078140-X
Printed in the United States of America
34567890   059   9876543

TO ESTER, LYNN,
ALAN, and JOHN

Foreword

About the Series

These case studies in cultural anthropology are designed to bring to students, in beginning and intermediate courses in the social sciences, insights into the richness and complexity of human life as it is lived in different ways and in different places. They are written by men and women who have lived in the societies they write about and who are professionally trained as observers and interpreters of human behavior. The authors are also teachers, and in writing their books they have kept the students who will read them foremost in their minds. It is our belief that when an understanding of ways of life very different from one's own is gained, abstractions and generalizations about social structure, cultural values, subsistence techniques, and the other universal categories of human social behavior become meaningful.

About the Author

George J. Klima is Associate Professor of Anthropology in the State University of New York at Albany, New York. He received his graduate training in Anthropology at Syracuse University and University of California, Los Angeles. He holds a Ph.D. from the University of California, Los Angeles, and has taught at Syracuse University, Long Beach State College, California State College, Los Angeles, University of California, Los Angeles, and University of Southern California. He is currently preparing a full-length color film on the Barabaig.

About the Book

The Barabaig of Tanzania, East Africa, numbering about 20,000 are one of the few surviving "cattle complex" people of what was only recently a widespread and classic cultural type in Africa. Barabaig culture in its traditional form survived both the German colonial administration and the British Mandate. Today, the independent government of Tanzania is implementing transformative change. The wearing of the traditional red-ochred toga has been banned, a basic subsistence shift from herding and seminomadism to sedentary horticulturalism is being programmed, ritual murder is severely punished, and hundreds of young people have been forcibly reeducated. Barabaig culture, as George Klima describes it, no longer exists in pristine form. This makes what he describes of special significance. Through his case study, students can acquire an understanding of one of the major forms of adaptation created by man in his millennia of cultural evolution.

It is fitting that the author should elect to make cultural ecology his major theme. He describes how the use of cattle and cattle products, as well as attitudes toward cattle, influence everything the Barabaig do. Milk and milk products, hides, drawn blood, cow dung, meat, and urine are all used. Property relations, sorcery, social status, child training, initiation, marriage, clan and lineage relations, settlement patterns, and intra- as well as inter-household relations all reflect the overall ecological adaptation the Barabaig have developed. The movement of cattle and men on the dusty plains during the dry season, the search for pasture, the use of water holes, and the seasonal alternation of wet and dry seasons are a rhythm of life.

This case study is at once a study of ecological adaptation among a specific people, a contribution to the understanding of a widespread cultural type in human history, and another significant testimony to both the diversity of human culture and the universality of human nature.

GEORGE AND LOUISE SPINDLER
General Editors

Phlox, Wisconsin
September 1969

Acknowledgments

I wish to express my gratitude to Dr. Louis S. B. Leakey who first suggested that I visit the Barabaig before going to study any other area of East Africa. I am forever grateful for his wise counsel.

My thanks go to the International African Institute and especially to Professor Daryll Forde, editor of the journal *Africa*, for his kind permission to use sections of my 1964 article, "Jural Relations Between the Sexes Among the Barabaig," *Africa*, Vol. 34, in this book.

I owe special thanks to my Barabaig assistant and companion, Gidasaid Mameng, who patiently endured my attempts to learn the ways of his people and was instrumental in bringing me closer to the Barabaig view of reality. To the many elders who discussed times past and problems of the present, I owe a personal debt which time cannot cancel.

George J. Klima

Albany, New York
September 1969

Contents

Herdsmen guarding cattle against predators.

Young men and girls performing a jumping dance. Dances at ritual gatherings last for hours and are one of the few occasions when large numbers of Barabaig congregate.

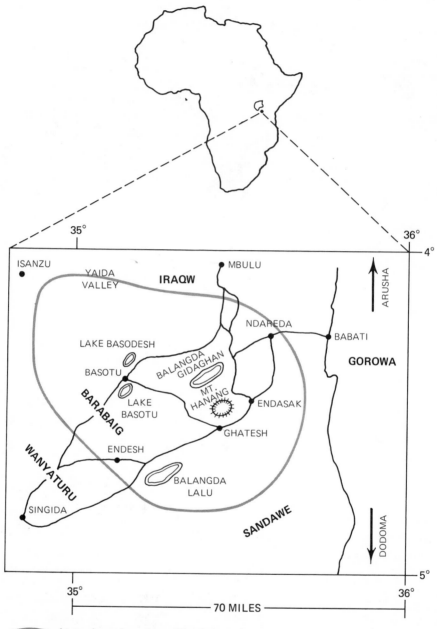

35° 36°

4°

ISANZU

YAIDA VALLEY IRAQW MBULU

ARUSHA

LAKE BASODESH NDAREDA BABATI

BASOTU BALANGDA GIDAGHAN GOROWA

BARABAIG LAKE BASOTU MT. HANANG ENDASAK

WANYATURU ENDESH GHATESH

BALANGDA LALU

SINGIDA

SANDAWE DODOMA

5°

35° 36°

|—————— 70 MILES ——————|

~~~~~ Approximate boundary of Barabaig territory

●   Small trading settlements (Somali)

⌒⌒⌒ Roads

BARABAIG Large letters indicate tribe

BASOTU Small letters indicate name of trading settlements

Introduction

TWO DAYS after I arrived in Barabaig country, I was approached by a group of men, one of whom demanded to know what I was doing in "his country." Being in a strange land and hearing a strange language, I hesitatingly began to speak in Ki-Swahili, the lingua franca of East Africa. Months later, I was to find out that the man who questioned me was the traditional paramount chief of the Barabaig—an enigmatic figure of whom the British administration of Tanganyika, East Africa, were only vaguely aware. His abrupt question caught me by surprise and I was about to answer him with some stock anthropological statement such as "I would like to study and record your customs so that your future children and the rest of the world will be able to know and understand how you lived." But looking at the scowling expression on the man's face, I quickly decided that he and his companions could not care less what would be known and remembered about them. So I answered him simply, saying, "I would like to live in your country."

My answer was as disarming as the original question, since neither he nor his companions had any experience with a European who was prepared to live among them. One of the chief's companions muttered something to him and they left as suddenly as they had appeared. Later, a man who had been translating my answers from Ki-Swahili to Ki-Barabaig so that the chief could understand, told me that I would be watched. I became an object of scrutiny and inquiry in the same way as the Barabaig became the focus of my attention. We studied each other. (I, of course, did not reciprocate when they looked inside my ears.)

I began my field work by walking around the country-side, familiarizing myself with the vegetation, the terrain, and the water supplies. People came to my camp to stare and to ask me questions in the Barabaig language—a language I began to learn from the questions they asked. After a few days, I knew how to greet people and how to answer simple questions with "yes" or "no." I was fortunate in obtaining the services of a Barabaig elder who spoke Ki-Swahili, and it was then that my fieldwork began in earnest. Gidasaid Mameng became my chief

1

informant, translator, and companion for much of the time I was with the Barabaig during my first field trip. He was extremely knowledgeable about his society and culture, being an influential elder and a member of one of the largest clans in Barabaig society. He was well liked by others, and with him accompanying me, I was allowed to witness and take part in many events that otherwise would have been impossible for an "outsider." His curiosity and "need to know" about Europeans was matched by my desire to learn about Barabaig culture.

After one month among the Barabaig, I was no longer a center of attraction, but people still had difficulty trying to place me somewhere within their conceptual scheme of things. A few Barabaig who had heard about missionaries speculated that I might be one of them and put me to assorted tests to ascertain this possibility. Others thought I might be a government spy sent to report on their activities. Again, more tests of very subtle design were performed in order to rule out or confirm the likelihood of my being a government agent. Having passed these tests, the Barabaig were still at a loss to assign me to some role other than "white man" or "outsider." After innumerable exchanges of greetings, during which the Barabaig asked for my clan affiliation, I decided to identify myself with the clan of my chief informant—a fortunate choice since the clan was one of the most respected, and relations with other clans were generally good. Now, for the first time, the Barabaig could locate me in their social structure and interact accordingly. However, I did not gain good rapport with the Barabaig until a few months later. I knew that I had come to be accepted by them when they became angry at me for some reason, such as not having a wad of tobacco handy when someone asked for it. Although some of my social and cultural errors were easily corrected, some of my thoughts and actions would remain forever alien to the Barabaig.

I arrived in Barabaig territory during the dry season, as planned, and was prepared to be as mobile as the Barabaig were with their homesteads and cattle-herds. A four-wheel drive Land Rover pickup truck with a camper unit in back was to be my home among the Barabaig. This rugged vehicle took me over boulder-strewn hills, thick mud, dense thorn-bush, and heavily fissured earth—places I had not imagined a car could go. It made possible the study of the Barabaig and their cattle as they moved from place to place. It also served as transport for barrels of water and tins of honey (carried in order to fulfill my kinship obligations to my adopted clan). Periodically, the pickup was transformed into an ambulance to take sick and dying people to distant mission and government hospitals. Without this physical mobility, I would not have been able to observe the wide spectrum of Barabaig life, with its social activity, its rituals, and its environmental problems.

The following account of Barabaig culture and society is based on field-work conducted during the periods, April 1955 through November 1956 and May 1958 through October 1959. Some of the patterns of behavior described in these pages may no longer exist but, hopefully, some of the solutions to the problems of biological and social existence among the Barabaig may be preserved, if only in the printed word.

During both periods of field work, I followed the standard procedure for field ethnography by collecting data through personal observation and participation in activities (when invited). I also utilized eight chief informants in different parts of Barabaig territory, as well as innumerable elders who volunteered to teach me Barabaig ways. No historical documents were available for consultation in matters dealing with the early history of the Barabaig prior to the advent of German colonial rule in 1891. The information in this study of Barabaig culture and society during pre-colonial times is based on information supplied by a number of elders who still remembered the traditional patterns of former years.

A number of different neighborhoods were mapped and a house-to-house census was made in order to study the changing social composition of neighborhoods. Genealogies were collected for the most part from male elders; women usually gave incomplete family histories and genealogies, either because of memory lapses, inaccurate knowledge, exigencies of domestic labor, or anxiety.

Use of motion-picture photography facilitated the recording of numerous rituals that would otherwise have had to be laboriously written down. At the same time, a large number of still pictures allowed me to count the number of people at various rituals, to identify them, and to study the many different cattle-brands found on Barabaig cattle. This was done in order to keep track of various livestock transfers that took place on special ritual and nonritual occasions (one of my main field problems in the study of the Barabaig). As my fieldwork advanced, I became more and more aware of some of the problems—environmental, social, and cultural—with which the Barabaig were struggling.

1

Cattle Complex and Ecology

Cattle Complex

ANTHROPOLOGISTS, following an example set by physical scientists, have attempted to devise various schemes for the classification of human phenomena. Numerous societies have been sorted out and labeled according to the degree to which they fit a particular category. Any society can be categorized differently, depending on the way it traces descent, determines kinship, establishes marriage residence, or extracts a living from its physical environment. In the latter category, the dominant mode of obtaining food is called a subsistence technique and the society is said to belong to a particular subsistence type, sharing this distinction with other societies having similar exploitative patterns of food-getting.

Some societies have mixed patterns of food-getting, which makes it difficult to assign them to a particular niche in a taxonomic or typological scheme. Such is the case with societies who herd domesticated animals. A class of cattle-herding society may include a wide range of societies extending from those who use cattle intensively and exclusively to furnish their sole diet to those societies with mixed patterns of food-getting in which cattle play only a minor role in the subsistence economy. For this reason, it is important to differentiate between those societies whose biological survival is strongly linked to the acquisition, maintenance, and control of cattle as compared with other societies that keep some cattle for purposes of prestige, or as a supplement to a diet that is mainly provided through other exploitative activities (such as the cultivation of domesticated plants).

Societies can be characterized as being cattle-herding societies on the basis of the contribution that cattle make to the total subsistence pattern of the people. Furthermore, cattle-herding societies usually exhibit something which anthropologists refer to as a "cattle-complex." A cattle-complex has been variously defined as (1) an extensive ritual usage of cattle, and (2) an emotional attach-

4

ment to or identification with cattle. I intend to use the term "cattle-complex" to mean a configuration or organization of behavior patterns whose existence depends upon cattle as a cultural and existential focus. These behavior patterns are problem-solution units which, directly or indirectly, have been influenced by the very nature of a strong reliance on domesticated animals for subsistence and basic biological survival. By extension, the possession of cattle also serves to satisfy a number of secondary or derived needs, such as the need for security (both short-term and long-term) and the need for personal recognition or social prestige. We can, therefore, speak of a cattle-complex as being "strongly" or "weakly" developed on the basis of whether there is an intensive and extensive use of cattle in the promotion and satisfaction of the biological and social life of a people.

Ecology

In the following study of the Barabaig, I shall utilize the concept of cultural ecology as a general framework within which the cattle-complex will be described and analyzed. Broadly stated, cultural ecology is the study of man's cultural adjustment to the organic and inorganic elements of his social and physical environments. This cultural adjustment can be seen in the kinds of solutions man devises to either eliminate or control within manageable limits the numerous problems arising from his social and physical life. Seen in this way, a society's cultural repertory consists of learned problem-solutions, which give its members both real and illusory control over events occurring in their social and physical environments.

Ecological adjustment of a society can be disrupted in a number of different ways. Changes in the physical environment may be the result of natural activity. Fluctuations in amount of rainfall may affect the growth of vegetation. Swarms of locusts and army-worms rapidly deplete vegetation. For the Barabaig, these and other changes seriously reduce the carrying capacity of the land to support animal and human populations and thus disrupt the delicate balance between organic and inorganic elements of the physical environment and Barabaig knowledge and action systems devised to establish this balance.

Human cultural activity may also disrupt a long-standing ecological adjustment through the introduction of new objects and ideas that change some aspect of the social and physical environments.

Man, through the use of his cultural repertory, solves certain problems, and at the same time creates new ones. A solution to a problem may start a chain-reaction leading to the creation of additional problems that may be of a greater magnitude than that of the original problem. Man, therefore, is both a problem-solving and problem-creating animal.

Certain things, such as birth, death, hunger, and personal recognition, arise as a universal condition of man, while other problems are specific and unique to particular societies. The Barabaig, by virtue of their reliance upon cattle for their subsistence, must devise solutions to protect their herds and must seek solutions to social problems arising out of their acquisition and control over domesticated animals. This is not to suggest that all social problems are directly or indirectly related to the keeping of cattle. On the contrary, social problems do occur as a result of faulty communication and other causes having no connection with the cattle-complex. However, any visitor to the Barabaig cannot fail to be impressed by the major expenditure of time, energy, and concern over cattle manifested in the daily behavior of the people. Cattle are the main topic of conversation and, indeed, many linguistic references to cattle are used to express thoughts and to communicate information.

Cattle are singularly important to the Barabaig in terms of making possible a biological and social existence. Without cattle, a person's chances of biological survival are lowered and his participation in social relations and relationships is severely curtailed. A man without cattle is a man without the necessary requisites for any sustained social interaction with others, since common interests are mainly concerned with the welfare of cattle. Cattle are the pivot or focal point around which a majority of thought and action patterns rotate and gravitate. An all-consuming interest in cattle places demands on the time, energy, skill, and knowledge of Barabaig cattle-herders. Every fluctuation in climate or vegetation is assessed in terms of its relevance for one's own cattle-herd. If the welfare of the cattle-herd is safe-guarded, it logically follows that the welfare of the people dependent upon the herd for their existence will be assured. So the fates of men and their cattle are inextricably intertwined in a dependency relationship that neither can willfully terminate without serious consequences.

2

The People and Their Cattle

The People

THE BARABAIG OF TANZANIA are the largest of several subtribes belonging to a widely dispersed ethnic group who call themselves Datog. Although accurate census data is not available, the Barabaig probably do not number in excess of 20,000 persons. Their language has been tentatively classified as belonging to the same Eastern Sudanic language group as the Nandi and Suk of Kenya.

In physical appearance, the Barabaig resemble the African somatic type known as Nilotic. They are of generally tall stature, with the men averaging about six feet in height, the women being a few inches shorter. Their skin color ranges from a light brown to black. A long thin nose and moderately everted lips make their facial features strikingly different from those of the surrounding tribes (the Bantu-speaking WaNyaturu and WaNyiramba, the bushmanoid Hadzapi, and the Sandawe [Hottentot]). Only their northern neighbors, the Iraqw, classified linguistically as Cushites, resemble the Barabaig but yet have some physical features (such as eye-shape) that set them apart from the Barabaig.

Various forms of body mutilation are practiced by the Barabaig. Scarification of the face is a common form of body decoration and is applied to both sexes. Using a knife, a number of small cuts are made in the skin in a circular fashion around each eye. Soot from burnt wood is rubbed into the incisions, producing permanent black keloid scars. Vertical cuts down each cheek may also be made. While many of the older generation are heavily scarified, fewer of the younger generation are, perhaps indicating that the practice may disappear in the near future.

Another common bodily mutilation is the piercing and extension of the lower part of the earlobes. When a child reaches ten years of age, the mother, or a specialist, will pierce the child's lower earlobes with a knife or arrow point and insert a twig. Larger wooden ear-plugs are inserted from time to time until an

Young girl with facial sacrification and distended ear-lobes. Brass neck coil and earrings are permanently worn.

ornamental plug can be worn. Males wear round ivory plugs, whereas females wear coiled brass rings with leather or small chain tassels attached. Unlike the scarification of the face, the distension of earlobes is universally practiced and does not appear to be losing popularity.

Modifications are also made in the appearance of teeth. When they are about ten years of age, both sexes must submit to an operation performed by a specialist who uses a small knife to cut the gums and to pry out the two lower incisor teeth. The Barabaig explain that this is done so that the child will not grow up with the "mouth of a donkey."

In pre-colonial times, Barabaig men wore a goat-skin or calf-skin cape fastened over one shoulder. This garment is only worn today when a man climbs upon a funerary monument in a dedication ceremony to his deceased father.

During the time of British rule, the skin cape was replaced by a length of cotton cloth, which the men draped over their shoulders and wrapped around their bodies in toga fashion. New white cotton cloth was bought from Somali or Arab traders who set up their small shops in trading centers along the two main dirt roads that trisect their land. Shortly after purchase, the white cotton cloth was smeared with a mixture of butter and red ochre, which served as a permanent dye. A pair of sandals made from cow-hide (or from old automobile tire casings) completed the wardrobe. In 1968, the independent government of Tanzania issued an edict banning the wearing of the *hangd,* the red-ochre-dyed toga, and today Barabaig men wear cotton shirts and shorts.

Changes in the dress of Barabaig women have also been proposed by the government. But the women resisted attempts by the former British government to make them wear cotton dresses, and the present government may have difficulty in convincing them to adopt western dress. Reasons for the women's strong objections to dress change are historical, magico-religious, and gynecological.

Barabaig women wear a leather skirt, *hanangwend,* made of strips of hide from calves, impala, goat, and sheep. These are sewn together to produce a wide-flaring pleated skirt that swirls around them when they walk or dance. A Barabaig myth states that Udameselgwa, a female deity and patroness of Barabaig women, taught the women how to make the skirt and assured them that if they followed insructions they would have many children. A special sheepskin panel is sewn in front of the skirt and is believed to promote fertility in the wearer, since the sheep is considered a sacred animal by the Barabaig. Thus, any attempt to persuade Barabaig women to discard their traditional leather skirt for a cotton dress will be met with strong resistance because of its magico-religious significance.

A leather cape, made of calf-skin or impala-skin, covers the upper part of the bodies of women and girls, but the cape is removed when working around the homestead. When carrying water, the women and girls fold their capes around a straw bundle and wrap it around their waist, forming a back cushion against the heavy weight of their water gourds. Young unmarried girls wear only the cape; the leather skirt is worn exclusively by married women and is one of the most visible means of identifying the marital status of a female. Every Barabaig girl must marry, whether or not she is physically desirable. Crippled, deformed, and demented girls must have a wedding in order for them to be eligible to wear the leather skirt designed by Udameselgwa.

Ornamentation of dress and body takes different forms in Barabaig men and women. Both sexes wear multicolored glass beads in strings around their necks, but only the women sew beads in geometric patterns on their garments. Skirts and capes used for ordinary daily wear have a minimum of decoration, but garments worn on ritual and festive occasions are decorated with intricate designs of beadwork sewn into the garments. Beaded decorations are the only examples of craftsmanship practiced by Barabaig women.

The Cattle

Barabaig cattle are of the zebu variety with a large hump over their shoulders and a loose fold of skin under their throats. Body height is about five feet at the shoulders. Horns vary, but generally do not exceed one and one-half feet in length. Animals with single colors—black, white, reddish-brown, and gray —are scarce and valued, while most cattle are of two-color combinations. Zebu cattle are hardy animals well-adapted to survive in a semiarid environment. Barabaig herders are faced with the necessity of seeing that their cattle both survive and thrive.

Other domesticated animals kept by the Barabaig include sheep, goats, and donkeys, although not every family herd will contain these supplemental animals. Donkeys are especially valuable as beasts of burden, being used to transport slabs of salt from certain salt beds to the homestead. These chunks of salt are put out for the cattle to use as salt-licks. When it is time to move a homestead or forage for food, donkeys carry most of the heavy loads.

Sheep are surrounded with an aura of sacredness because of their inherent docility, and are used as sacrificial animals on certain ritual occasions. Goats are used mainly as a meat and milk supply, being a valuable supplement to the milch cows—especially when the milk yield of the cows is low during the dry season.

Dogs roam around the homestead, being mainly scavengers rather than household pets. They are not trained to assist in herding livestock, but are used to lick away the bowel movements of babies.

Barabaig cattle cannot be classed as good dairy animals. Cows are brought to their food, rather than having food brought to them. Long walks to find sufficient grazing during the dry season produce a state of physical exhaustion in the animals, and this affects their ability to lactate. Poor nutrition and in-breeding also lower the milk yield of most cows. One cow yields about 4 to 6 pints of milk each day, but since a Barabaig cow lactates only when it has a calf, this milk yield must be shared by calf and people alike. Calves suckle for about seven months.

Calves are kept separate from their mothers during the day, but are united in the evening. Cows with calves are usually placed in a separate section of the homestead, away from the rest of the herd. At night, the dam is led back to the cattle corral containing the bulls and cows without calves, while its calf is brought inside a compartment of a wife's hut.

Cows are milked twice each day, but generally yield more milk in the morning when they have rested during the night than in the evening after they have been walking all day in search of grasses. Deception is necessary in order to milk the cows. Women generally do the milking chores, but husbands sometimes help—especially when a wife is sick. The milker holds the calf's head between his legs and stands near the cow. The cow gets the impression that the calf is at the udder and let's down it's milk, which is caught in a milk gourd. After a quantity of milk is obtained, the calf is allowed to finish suckling. If there is a serious milk shortage in the household, all of the milk will be drawn into gourds and then a measured amount will be given to the calf. However, the milker must make sure that the calf receives sufficient milk or it may die. At times, some Barabaig are faced with the problem of who needs milk the most, the family or the calves. If the family herd is to grow in numbers, calves must be guarded against starvation, thirst, and disease.

In order to prevent the young stock from dying of thirst during the dry season, women of the homestead carry large water gourds (holding approximately 5 gallons) strapped to their backs and trudge with their loads from the crater lakes to their homes. Many women have a round-trip of two miles or more to the lakes and back every two days in order for the homestead to have sufficient water for the family and the young livestock.

Death of a calf may precipitate a crisis in the homestead. A cow without its calf will cease letting down its milk. Faced with the probability that a milch cow will stop lactating, the Barabaig resort to more deception. Straw is stuffed into the skin of a dead calf so that it resembles the animal. Salt water is sprinkled on the back of the dummy calf. When milking time nears, the milch cow is allowed to lick the skin of its dead calf and this starts the cow lactating again. In this way, the milk supply is protected until the cow can give birth to another calf, which can usually occur each year.

Household Uses of Cattle Products

Cow's milk, prepared in a number of different ways, is the traditional food of the Barabaig, but its importance in providing subsistence for each family has been steadily diminishing. Milk has never been in steady supply for most Barabaig, except during the rainy season when adequate grazing stimulates lactation in cows. While Barabaig cattle are not an entirely unreliable source of food, their fluctuating milk yield does periodically induce concern and anxiety in those people who are most reliant upon their animals for their subsistence. Also, reliance upon a commodity, such as milk, which cannot be stored or preserved easily, creates problems of utilization, but only in cases where a definite surplus can be accumulated. Most Barabaig, except the wealthy cattle-owners, are not faced with problems of food surpluses.

Food preferences differ between the sexes, with men preferring to drink raw cow's milk whereas curdled or churned milk is the choice of women. Butter is produced by separating the butterfat from the watery liquid and shaking it in a gourd until thick. A clarified liquid butter, or ghee, is also made by boiling butter Butter is essentially a cooking medium mixed with meat. But on ritual occasions it becomes an anointment placed on people's heads and rubbed into skin garments. It is also used on non-ritual occasions to keep leather garments and harnesses from drying out.

Milk is mixed with cow's blood and either drunk raw or cooked together to form a thick paste, the latter being the preferred method. Blood is extracted from an animal, usually a bull, by shooting a blocked arrow into the jugular vein of the neck, the spurting blood being caught in an open gourd bowl. Arrow points are wrapped in thin leather strips so that only about one inch of the tip protrudes beyond the binding. A leather tourniquet is tightened around the bull's neck, distending the jugular vein and thus providing a target for the arrow, which is shot from a bow. After about one gallon of blood is extracted, the tourniquet is loosened and the jugular vein pinched shut by finger pressure. The animal is released and may not be "tapped" again for some time, depending upon the size of the herd and the supply of milk. The technique of extracting blood from a living animal is similarly practiced by other East African cattle-herding societies.

When a cow or bull dies of old age, disease, or in sacrifice, the meat is eaten and, indeed, appreciated by the family. Cattle are not used as a regular meat supply, but when an animal dies, almost every portion will be utilized for some purpose. Although chunks of beef may be roasted on sticks near a fire, more often the meat is boiled in water or in a mixture of blood and butter.

Meals are eaten twice a day during the dry season and three times a day during the rainy season. If the cattle herd is scheduled to travel to distant grazing areas, dry season meals begin at 6 A.M. or earlier. The evening meal, at 6 P.M. starts after all of the livestock are in their corral. During the rainy season, cattle are pastured at 8 A.M. and return near the kraal at noon and then graze around the neighborhood until dusk. It is a time when people and their animals no longer struggle for food.

Extracting blood from a young bull. After the desired quantity of blood is obtained, the leather strap around the neck is released and the jugular vein is pinched shut with finger pressure.

From the hides of Barabaig cattle, a wide variety of leather goods is produced. Women's leather garments are fashioned from calf-skin, which is made supple by soaking for a number of days in a pot of human urine. Before putting it to soak, the hide is first staked out on the ground to stretch, then put on a wooden frame where it is scraped clean of hair and flesh. Hides of older animals are used to cover bed frames or are cut into pieces to make grain sacks, sandals, and assorted straps used for tying and binding purposes.

Horns are converted into receptacles or instruments. Long cattle horns are especially prized as drinking horns or cups and are eagerly sought after when the honey beer is passed around. A drinker, using a cattle horn for a cup, must finish its contents in a single draught. Small horns are hollowed out and covered with leather and beadwork (an attractive tobacco pouch). Finely powdered tobacco in the form of snuff is stored in these containers and offered to other young men and to girl friends. Tobacco is inhaled in the nostrils by women, young girls, and young men, but older men generally place a wad under their lower lip and chew it. Some small cattle horns are also used by curers to draw blood away from an incision made on a swollen part of their patient's body.

Cow dung is used as a binding agent in the construction of huts and funerary monuments. Dung is not used for fuel since there is generally no scarcity of firewood in most sections of Barabaig territory. Cow urine is used to wash out milk gourds and is also applied as an antiseptic to cuts and scratches. There is hardly a part or product of a cow that is not utilized by the Barabaig in their domestic life.

Other Foods

Cultivation of maize has been increasingly contributing to the subsistence of the Barabaig but, so far, land under cultivation consists mostly of small plots of one-quarter to one-half an acre. But these do not produce enough maize to feed a small family from one harvest to the next. In times of food shortage, goats or a young bull are bartered for maize and millet obtained in barter from neighboring horticultural tribes. Maize has an advantage over milk as a staple food in that it can be stored for long periods of time and used when needed, whereas milk and milk products have only a short-term provision basis. However, storage of maize creates many new problems. Maize cobs can be thrown on a hut roof or tied in bunches and hung in a tree. When more maize is cultivated, these methods are no longer suitable and some form of bin or container is then necessary. Corn-cribs built above the ground or a large cylinder moulded out of wood ash and human urine are methods of storage borrowed from Iraqw and Gorowa horticulturalists, the northern neighbors of the Barabaig. However, the construction of large grain receptacles reduces a family's physical mobility when it is time to move the homestead and, indeed, on many occasions, homesteads in the paths of raging grass fires have lost their entire supply of stored grain. While reliance on cereal grain to provide subsistence is increasing among the Barabaig, there is a general reluctance to become a stationary, sedentary population, rooted to the soil, which must be "scratched" in order to grow food. The present government of Tanzania is forcing a program of change on the Barabaig, and it will only be a matter of time before these seminomadic cattle-herders will be transformed into sedentary horticulturalists.

Wild honey has provided the Barabaig with a ready source of energy when eaten raw but it has more often been reserved for the brewing of honey-beer, *ghamung*, an alcoholic beverage which has magico-religious significance for the Barabaig. It is considered to be of sacred origin because the secret of its preparation is believed to have been handed down by God, *Aset*, to mortal man in the person of Ghambideg. Ghambideg, a legendary figure, then instructed his children, who were twins and capable of full speech at birth, to tell others to use honey-beer on all ritual occasions. Thus, mythological and supernatural validation reinforces the Barabaig belief that honey-beer is a sacred drink made known to Man through divine revelation.

Women are allowed to eat raw honey, but the brewing and drinking of honey-beer are considered to be the exclusive rights of men. Some elderly women claim to have secretly tasted honey-beer on a number of occasions during their lifetime.

Large gourds are obtained from neighboring horticultural tribes and when converted into brewing-gourds, *geskweg,* become endowed with special magical powers. Some of these gourds are very old and have gained additional magical and mystical properties from having been used for generations by influential elders who have long joined the multitude of ancestral spirits who now watch over the people.

Game animals, large and small, provide an additional source of food, but one that is not relied upon to any great extent. Animals are either stalked or hunted from blinds constructed near lakes where most animals go to drink during the dry season. During the rainy season, some large animals, such as giraffe, zebra, and wildebeest, become mired in deep mud-holes and are speared. More often, bow and poisoned arrow are used to hunt wild game. Arrow poison is made by a subgroup of the Datog (known as Bisiyed) who boil down the cut wood from a special tree and extract a powerful blood poison, a cardiacglycocide, which topples the largest of animals in a matter of minutes. Men, in the heat of chase, have been known to trip over their arrows and fall dead in minutes. Hunting is one activity of Barabaig males that is hazardous and tends to reduce the numbers of living males.

Mutual Dependence of Man and Cattle

Just as the Barabaig rely upon cattle for their subsistence and other culturally meaningful patterns, so their cattle rely upon the Barabaig. The Barabaig provide the necessary protection against starvation, thirst, disease, and human and animal predators without which their chances for biological survival would be practically nonexistent. The herders bring their animals to grasses, water, and salt, based on their knowledge and information of their country. Domesticated animals left to themselves in a semiarid and disease-ridden environment would not survive for long. Their masters prevent them from entering tsetse-fly infested areas where the grasses are tall and tempting, or blundering into a deep mudhole, or falling prey to lion, leopard, or wild dog. Cattle require the technology and intelligence of Barabaig herding, and the Barabaig require the subsistence and social advantages gained from their animals. Both are locked in a dependency relationship from which neither can easily separate.

Cattle herds owned by the Barabaig vary in numbers from a few head to several hundred head of cattle, with the "average" herd estimated at about 70 animals. No accurate statistics on Barabaig cattle-holdings are available since herd-owners are evasive and secretive about the actual head count of their herds. Herds are divided, especially during the dry season, and many herds move about so frequently that an accurate count is not possible. A wealthy cattle owner, according to the Barabaig, is a man with approximately 500 head of cattle, four or more wives, many sons, and a few daughters.

Increase in the size of a cattle herd solves certain problems while creating others. With more animals in the family herd, especially cows, the possibility of having more milch cows and more milk is increased. Up to a certain point, the surplus of milk in a small household is a highly desirable situation, with both the family and calves being well fed. However, if the size of the herd increases at a greater rate than the size of the family, the family may be well fed but may also have difficulty in herding larger numbers of cattle. Difficulty does not lie in herding livestock so that they graze together in a group, but in keeping one's herd separated from another herd when both herds happen to converge on a lake shore at the same time. During the dry season, when cattle are watered at crater lakes, a great deal of congestion of herds takes place with inevitable mix-ups and stock losses resulting from the confusion. Many a herd has returned to a homestead minus or plus a few animals. Tracking down stray animals that have disappeared for one reason or another, such as faulty herding practices, consumes time and energy and may prove unsuccessful.

Increasing the number of herdsmen in order to more efficiently control a large herd can be accomplished in a number of ways. A young boy from a family poor in livestock may be hired with the promise of payment of one cow as his wages. More often, a man with a large herd has a greater opportunity to marry a second or third wife and thus acquire a new family member and herder. For the payment of one cow to the family of his intended bride, a man can obtain a wife. By judicious manipulation of a family herd, through stock transfers, loans to relatives and friends, and the division of a large herd into two parts, the size of a family herd can be kept within manageable limits and, at the same time, provide a steady supply of milk for the homestead.

When the size of the family increases at a greater rate than the size and ability of the family herd to support it, a situation of potential famine exists in the homestead. Kinsmen can be relied upon to supply a milch cow or two as a temporary "stop-gap" measure, but if they are similarly affected by a food shortage because of their herds' inability to provide sufficient milk, the kinsmen consider their own families' welfare first and kinship obligations secondly.

Families with small herds are more likely to turn to nontraditional means of supplementing their diet than families with large cattle-holdings that provide adequate nourishment in milk for the people and their smaller stock. Staunch traditionalists are generally those cattle-owners with large herds who can easily subscribe and conform to traditional Barabaig values and attitudes concerning the herding of livestock and the pastoral life.

3

Building Up a Herd

Strategies

EVERY BARABAIG HERD-OWNER seeks to acquire, maintain, and improve upon his control over the social and physical environments in which he finds himself. In this respect, he is no different from other individuals in other societies. He differs in the means, both empirical and supernatural, by which he hopes and expects to achieve this control. Simply stated, the degree of control a person has is measured by the difference between what he intends to do and what he actually accomplishes. Given a capricious physical environment, it is almost inevitable that a Baraband's attempt at mastery will fall short of expectations. Yet, he continues to probe for that elusive variable, or variables, which might spell the difference between success and failure. He sees other herd-owners enjoying more success than he and it confirms his belief that through personal striving the possible can become the actual.

The challenges of his social and physical environments produce in him a state of readiness to act swiftly and decisively. Of four modes of dealing with problems—attack, retreat, compromise, and no action—he more often chooses to attack a problem with those resources which are immediately available. For this reason and others, he is present-time oriented and grasps opportunities when they arise. Surrounded by predators, both human and animal, and an unpredictable physical environment, Barabaig herd-owners must resort to shifting strategies in order to protect their herds and their families. This is not to suggest that a Barabaig herd-owner is constantly experimenting with different herding techniques for the purpose of gaining greater control and hence predictability over events affecting the welfare of his herd and family. He finds himself involved in a "high-risk" game of life in which he is pitted against an uncompromising environment and fellow competitors. In these physical and social situations, flexibility rather than strict adherence to old patterns is the key to survival. Changes in physical and social environments force the Barabaig to choose between a limited number of alternative courses of action. The cycle of herd-building and

17

depletion is experienced by every herd-owner and is partially a reflection of his individual responses to situations of choice in the past. It is not difficult to observe Barabaig herding strategies in action. A more difficult task is the study of feedback and correction of faulty choices and performances as a result of incomplete knowledge and information about certain situations upon which Barabaig herd-owners have acted. How have they herded their animals through time and space?

Many of the strategies employed by Barabaig herd-owners to deal with problems arising out of their pastoral life are culturally shared, although individual variations in choice and performance lead to different outcomes. Problems of water and grass shortage cannot be handled in the same way as problems concerned with the health, fertility, and theft of cattle. Some of these problems are more amenable to adequate solution than others, given the knowledge of physical environment and animal husbandry the Barabaig possess.

The Problem of Land

During the dry season, Barabaig herdsmen are almost constantly faced with making decisions about moving their cattle herds around the territory in search of grass and browsing for their livestock. With the end of the rainy season, cattle herds begin to range wider in their grazing and soon deplete the areas nearest to the homesteads. The pattern of feeding changes from a sedentary or almost stationary one to long trips to places where grass is still available. Seasonal movement of people and animals in response to climate and vegetational changes is referred to by ecologists as transhumance. It is a pattern familiar to the Barabaig and many other African cattle-herding societies. Transhumance may be complicated by geographic and political factors, as it is in the case of the Barabaig.

Barabaig tribal territory is located roughly between longitudes 35° E and 36° E and latitudes 4° S and 5° S. Within this area there are open, rolling plains that undulate within an altitude range of 4000 to 6000 feet above sea level, intersected by the Rift Wall that extends in a north-south direction. Thus, the Barabaig are divided, topographically, into two sections—those who live in the Rift Valley and others who are located at a higher altitude above the Rift Wall. While the Rift Wall, in places, may extend several hundred feet upward in a near vertical position, there are breaks along the wall that permit Barabaig herdsmen to bring their cattle down along well-worn paths to the valley floor and back up again as grazing possibilities change. However, most Barabaig, through long-standing habit, are either permanent residents of the valley floor or the higher ground. Occasionally, some herd-owners try to improve their fortunes by moving down into the valley or up to the top of the escarpment but, generally, herd-owners prefer to reside in territory they know best. Whether they live in the valley or above, their movement about the country is oriented spatially with reference to a prominent landmark. A solitary, extinct volcano, Mount Hanang, which rises 11,215 feet above sea level, dominates the landscape and serves as a point of orientation (like a north star) for the Barabaig in their journeys to distant places within their territory.

With the imposition of colonial rule, first by the Germans and later under British Mandate, the Barabaig have been relegated to fixed political boundaries that have caused them considerable problems in their ecological adjustment between the requirements of their cattle and the carrying capacity of the land to sustain life. Confined to a limited territory of approximately 2500 square miles, cattle-herders have become increasingly hard-pressed to find adequate grazing for their herds. Periodically, they have had to move into peripheral lands held by other tribes, thereby causing serious border disputes that threatened to break out into intertribal warfare but for the intervention of the Tanganyikan government who sent a police force into the area to restore law and order. Invariably, Barabaig cattle-herders were forced to move back within their own tribal borders. In this way, the government of Tanganyika promoted tribal separatism in the interest of political stability.[1]

At the time the government adopted a policy of territorial containment of the Barabaig, it instructed its appointed chief and headmen of Barabaig wards to turn back any settlers of other tribes who might venture into Barabaig territory. At first, heeding the complaints of Barabaig herd-owners, the government appointed chief and headmen forced some Iraqw families who were recent settlers to return to Iraqw territory. But it soon became apparent that the flow of Iraqw families into Barabaig land could not be stopped. Besides, the process of infiltration had already begun some years previous through means other than encroachment through herding activity. The following is a post facto account of Iraqw infiltration narrated to me by a number of Barabaig elders reflecting upon a process which, at the time it was occurring, continued unrecognized by the Barabaig until it became widespread and irreversible.

Traditionally, young Barabaig men have had to rely on their parents and relatives for donations of livestock to be used to obtain a bride. Bridewealth, the transfer of valued property from the family of the bridegroom to the family of the bride, was necessary before a young man could marry. A few young men from poor families went to work as herdsmen for wealthy Barabaig herd-owners and in return for one or more years of labor were given stock that could be used for bridewealth. In some instances, young men even married the daughters of these wealthy men. More often, the young men were economically dependent upon their parents for a long time before they could get the necessary cows for the marriage to take place. One day, some young men discovered that it was possible to marry without paying bridewealth. They learned of a custom whereby young Iraqw girls upon becoming pregnant, or suffering a miscarriage, were forced to live as an outcast in a hut isolated from family and friends. The Iraqw fear blood and the fetus of unmarried girls. Food is cautiously brought to the outcast during the period of her seclusion. Some Barabaig men took ad-

---

[1] References to various governments will be: German East Africa (German colonial Government) 1891–1918; Tanganyika Territory (British Mandate under the League of Nations and later a trust territory under the UN) 1918–1961; Tanzania (Independent African government) 1961– .

vantage of this situation by offering to marry the girls, thus cutting short their social isolation. They did not have to pay bridewealth to the girls' parents because of their ritually polluted condition. Brought back to Barabaig territory, the Iraqw girl would ask her husband for permission to cultivate a small plot of land to grow some maize or millet as a supplemental to the family's diet. Her husband usually did not object to this suggestion since his wife came from a horticultural society and knew how to use a hoe. Besides, if she wanted to dig up the soil, that was her affair. After a while, the Barabaig husband acquired a taste for maize and millet porridge as a daily meal and even helped his wife cultivate the now expanded gardens. He also recognized the advantage of growing cereal grains that could be stored and used to offset any deficiency in the milk yield of his cows. Maize and millet became more culturally acceptable, although some staunch traditionalists continued to rely almost exclusively on their cows for subsistence. They looked with disdain upon others scratching the ground for food. These traditionalists were usually wealthy cattle-owners whose herds were large enough to insure a steady supply of milk. Barabaig women began to imitate their Iraqw co-wives or neighbors and soon there was hardly a neighborhood that did not have at least one cultivated field. Growing maize and millet became a hedge against food shortages that periodically affected most Barabaig families. Cattle were no longer considered a reliable source of food, but their value was not lessened appreciably because of their important functions in the social, economic, and political life of the Barabaig.

As more young Barabaig men married Iraqw outcasts and brought them to live in Barabaig territory, more and more land was placed under cultivation. Iraqw men began to visit their married sisters and stayed to help cultivate larger fields. Other Iraqw men brought cattle with them and married Barabaig girls. With the influx of Iraqw cultivators and cattle-herders, the availability of grazing area for Barabaig cattle was substantially reduced. Government policy of maintaining tribal integrity through enforced territoriality became more difficult to implement and was finally abandoned. Iraqw cattle-herders, now freed of governmental restraint, penetrated deeply into Barabaig territory in a southerly direction, coming to a stop at the border marking the political administrative boundaries of the Mbulu and Singida Districts. There was hardly a neighborhood that did not have Iraqw cattle-herders.

In and around many of the trading settlements, such as Ndareda, Endasak, and Ghatesh, heavy concentrations of Iraqw settlers pushed many Barabaig out to seek less congested land where they could graze their cattle unobstructed by cultivated fields. Iraqw settlers felt protected by the presence of a small detachment of Tanganyikan police. In some cases, Barabaig cattle caused damage to crops in Iraqw gardens and the presence of livestock and gardens proved to be sources of conflict between Barabaig and Iraqw. Some Barabaig with small herds remained and started to cultivate small plots of about ¼ to ½ acres, while the owners of larger herds moved away to retain their strong values and attitudes regarding the ability of their livestock to support and supply the family with food. Migration, the traditional solution to grazing and, more recently, political problems became the order of the day. However, the Barabaig soon learned that there were few places left where they could bring their cattle without inciting some hostile opposition.

Reduction of grazing area as a result of extensive cultivation and increase in the number of herds put greater demands on the carrying capacity of the land to support the cattle population. Some land had always been unsuitable or unavailable for grazing, being either thick bush infested with tsetse fly, rocky areas, ravines, or large salt flats. With the political administrative boundaries remaining unchanged and the cattle population increasing in numbers, problems of over-grazing and soil erosion reached a magnitude requiring some governmental intervention. Culling programs designed to reduce the number of livestock, together with the monetary inducement of the cattle market, were steps which the government took to ease the pressure on local vegetation and soil. These programs were less than successful as long as the government vacillated in its conception of the role of Barabaig society in the larger national economy.

Government officials were faced with the problem of deciding whether to consider the Barabaig as stock-raisers and thus perpetuate their strongly-entrenched "cattle complex" and ethnic identity or to systematically deplete the cattle herds and thus prepare them for acceptance of change to a different subsistence activity. This would be horticulture, which would presumably make them more governable and more easily assimilated into neighboring horticultural societies.

The Problem of Water

One of the major problems that must be solved in order to achieve an ecological adjustment to the physical environment is the availability of water. The Barabaig live in a semiarid environment where rainfall is never plentiful, averaging about twenty inches per year throughout most of the area. It is considerably higher in the vicinity of Mount Hanang, where cloud cover is more often present. Locally, the year has two distinct seasons—a wet season, which usually extends from about November to May with a short interruption of the rains in February, and a dry season from May to October. Droughts occur every few years and cause considerable suffering among the Barabaig, their cattle, and numerous wild animals sharing the same water supplies.

No permanent rivers flow through Barabaig territory, although there are a few very small streams that flow down from Mount Hanang. Small springs also gush from the side of the Rift Wall, but these are low in output and many dry up during the dry season. Small crater lakes are the only permanent supply, except for a few wells, located in low-lying areas, which are dug and owned by individuals. In these areas, cattle are watered by the laborious method of hauling up leather or tin buckets of water and dumping them in an open trough or ditch from which the cattle drink. Crater lakes are filled seasonally by rainwater that runs through a number of ravines into the lakes. There are no outlets for these lakes and therefore the water is stagnant for most of the year. Water levels at many of the crater lakes may fall to low, critical proportions following a year of poor rains or drought. When this occurs, all animal life in the area is seriously affected, especially in some crater lakes, such as the one known as Basotu, where the water level drops so low that the backs of hippo living in the lake are exposed to the sun's rays. Standing in shallow water, the hippo have a difficult time trying to submerge themselves in order to prevent their hides from cracking and peeling.

As the dry season advances, not only does the water level in crater lakes drop each day, but the water itself becomes more foul and alive with organisms. More and more animals now depend upon the dwindling water supply for their very lives. During the day, between the hours of 10 A.M. to 2 P.M., Barabaig herdsmen bring their livestock to water in an almost continuous procession. Women come to fill large water gourds and carry them on their backs to homesteads that may be located at a distance of more than 2 miles from the lake. In late afternoon, thousands of guinea-fowl race toward the lakes to quench their thirst. At night, under cover of darkness, a different and stranger procession takes place. Large herds of wild animals that have been grazing in the hot, open plains begin to file toward the lake. Hundreds of zebra, wildebeest, impala, gazelles, giraffe, and other animals, large and small, converge on the lakes to drink. Most of these animals have had to wait all day before they could use the lakes because they fear the heavy and continuous traffic of Barabaig and their cattle herds during the daylight hours.

On higher ground, the red soil turns to dust under the relentless pressure of sun, wind, and the hooves of thousands of animals. Large cattle herds stir up dust clouds which can be seen rising over one hundred feet in the air. Some Barabaig men can make accurate guesses about the ownership of a particular herd approaching a lake just by watching the length of the column of dust kicked up by the cattle. The statement, "Here comes Ganak" (the owner of a herd numbering several hundred head) is made in a matter-of-fact way even before the herd itself becomes visible. There are not many herds capable of raising such dust clouds. Herds of this size help to attract attention to the wealth of their owners. The name of a wealthy man reaches into every corner of Barabaig territory.

Before the first rains arrive, there is apprehension among the Barabaig. In every neighborhood, small groups of men sit huddled under shade trees discussing the prospects of rain. "Where is the rain?" "The rain is lost." "The rain is near." Lightning flashes may be seen to the west. Some dark clouds appear on the horizon, then disappear. Thunder rumbles in the distance but still no rain. Elders of the neighborhood of Gidamambura hold a council meeting to decide on a rain-making ritual. They command some young men to bring a sheep to the crater lake and dip it in the water, making sure that when it is taken out it shakes itself so vigorously that drops of water will fly in all directions. The sheep is then taken back to the homestead where it is strangled. Strips of skin are taken from the sheep and hung in trees (preferably fig trees) around the neighborhood and the nearby lake. At the lake, neighborhood women gather to sing religious songs to elicit the aid of ancestral spirits who are in close association with God, *Aset*, and can therefore intercede on their behalf. The neighborhood is alive with activity directed toward the promotion of rain. One elder has had a dream that the impending rains will be so heavy that birds will be killed in the trees; animals and people will die. His prophetic dream prompts a meeting of the neighborhood elders who decide to sacrifice another sheep to prevent this calamity. Distracted by noise, eyes turn skyward to watch a jet airliner streak across the clear sky. Discussion on the organization of animal sacrifice resumes. A growing anxiety settles over the community, but the people are together— trying to solve the problem of rain.

First rains are light, intermittent showers. With the coming of heavy rains, the lakes suddenly become deserted. Water fills the ravines and open depressions everywhere. Small marshes and lakes appear in the low-lying basins where previously the "black-cotton" clay soil lay cracked and fissured. The air becomes filled with the smell of new vegetation sprouting up from the barren ground. New grass means new life and energy for all. Soon the cattle will grow fat and sleek and milk will be plentiful again. It is a time of great happiness and the Barabaig begin to arrange certain rituals that have had to be postponed because of a lack of butter. The gloom and quiet desperation surrounding the struggle of the cattle-herders to find grazing for their livestock is dispelled with the coming of the rains. Rapid growth of new grasses allows some families to move back to their old neighborhoods while others seek out relatives in new neighborhoods. It is now possible to move homesteads into areas formerly uninhabitable because of a lack of water. The constant vigilance over the welfare of the herd that consumed so much time and energy during the dry season is lessened but the tall grass now hides the lion and the problem of water has been eclipsed by the problem of predators.

The Problem of Grazing

Locating a reliable water supply and adequate grazing are two problems with which the Barabaig, as a pastoral society, must contend every year. As the herds of livestock increase, fostered by governmental programs of cattle-dipping and inoculations against bovine pleuropneumonia, rinderpest, hoof and mouth disease, rift valley fever, and sleeping sickness, the grazing areas become overcrowded and overgrazed. Annual grass fires, accidentally and deliberately set,[2] burn out thousands of acres of valuable grazing area and sometimes destroy homesteads in their path. Periodically, grazing areas are reduced by invasions of millions of army-worms that destroy the valuable grass. In response to these conditions, some Barabaig families move their herds into border areas and come into conflict with neighboring tribesmen. Encroachment on land held by other tribes often causes serious border disputes that have to be resolved by action of the Tanganyika Police.

During the dry season, the grazing pattern followed is one in which two routes or orbits are alternated. One day the cattle are grazed in a direction away from the water supply and brought back to the homestead at night. The

---

[2] Fires are set to burn out coarse weeds and dry grasses that cut the mouths of grazing cattle. Although this firing destroys edible grass, it also helps to promote new grass growth. Firing of grass becomes destructive when fires rage unchecked and spread into neighboring grazing areas.

next day they graze out from the homestead to the water supply, usually arriving at the lakes between the hours of 10 A.M. and 2 P.M. It is during this period that the greatest congestion of traffic occurs, with large herds converging on the lake making it difficult for the herders to keep their livestock separated. Sometimes cattle stray and join other herds, or two herds merge which then requires considerable effort to sort out stock belonging to each herd. At this season, livestock are watered every second day, entering the water and drinking for about five minutes, which seems to be sufficient for their needs. Cattle also require salt. The Barabaig solve this problem by bringing their herds to one of the many natural salt lakes scattered at various points throughout the territory. In areas where salt is not available, neighbors organize a salt caravan to one of two major salt lakes (Balangda Lalu and Balangda Gidaghan) located in Barabaig territory. Large slabs of salt are loaded in sacks and tied on the backs of donkeys, the only animals used by the Barabaig for transporting loads when they forage or move homesteads.

Grazing is restricted to the open grassland area because of heavy infestation of tsetse fly in the wooded sections around the periphery of the tribal territory. Near the end of the dry season, some Barabaig herders may bring their cattle to graze these areas but most herders will not risk exposing their herds to bovine trypanosomiasis—the sleeping sickness affecting cattle.

Grazing becomes more difficult as the dry season approaches its fourth or fifth month. Grasses are sparse and when available are so coarse as to cut the mouths of cattle. Some cattle even attempt to stand up in order to eat leaves from small trees. Large numbers of sheep and goats reduce available grazing for cattle since they, as well as hundreds of wild animals, are competing against cattle for the same dwindling supply of grass. However, sheep and goats have some advantages over their bovine competitors since they can eat leaves and coarse weeds and can graze closer to the ground. The Barabaig practice of keeping goats and sheep leads to greater soil erosion as a result of the grass being cropped shorter than is the case when cattle graze. However, goats and sheep are not part of the cattle complex but are kept as a meat supply. Not many Barabaig families have herds of sheep and goat, although there appears to be a trend toward greater reliance on these animals as a source of food and, more recently, income.

One strategy employed by owners of large herds is division of homestead and family herd. Two or more homesteads may be constructed at some distance from each other and the household and livestock divided. While the head of the household does not legally own all of the animals that are quartered within the confines of his homestead, nevertheless, he does exercise control over affairs related to the welfare of the family herd. The locations of homesteads are determined by the male head of the household. His choice of location will be influenced by ecological and sociological factors. He must weigh his knowledge of availability of water and grazing against social considerations of moving into a neighborhood where he has relatives or in-laws. If he is the head of a large polygynous family, with stock-holdings which exceed two hundred head of cattle, it is his responsibility to decide whether the herd should remain together or whether, because of poor grazing, the family herd should be divided into two herds, sending one herd 5 or more miles away to be quartered at a secondary homestead. He then selects the wives and children who will occupy the new homestead. Usually the second wife is placed in charge of the secondary home-stead and she exercises nominal authority over the co-wives who accompany her to the new location. The husband will then alternate between the two home-steads, spending approximately equal time in each kraal.

Decisions to keep the family and its herd intact, or to subdivide them, are periodically made by wealthy Barabaig, according to environmental conditions and personal knowledge. Since the welfare of the people is bound so inex-tricably to the welfare of the cattle, the geographic separation of the family is a minor consideration as compared to the possibilities of finding better grazing for the cattle elsewhere, thus relieving the kind of competition for grazing which would otherwise ensue as a result of keeping the herd intact.

Each family has its own body of knowledge and information upon which it bases its decisions. It is a self-sufficient economic unit with a cultural repertory not quite like that of any other family. Thus, for example, in the Basotu ward during the dry season, Gidaleid usually elects to separate his herd of 250 head of cattle into two groups, sending one herd in a westerly direction toward the valley known as the Yaida—a place where rains and new vegetation sometimes appear earlier than in the Basotu area. Since other cattle-owners may have similar plans, Gidaleid does not send his entire herd to the Yaida. Another herd-owner, Gidamesh, from a different neighborhood of the Basotu ward, also con-trols about 250 head of cattle. But, unlike Gidaleid, he is habitually reluctant to divide his herd in the dry season, electing to take his chances in the Basotu ward or the adjacent wards. Whether Gidaleid, by dividing his large herd in the dry season, is practicing a more efficient method of pastoralism than Gidamesh, who chooses to keep his large herd together, is problematical. The idea of "spreading the risk" by dividing the herd so that at least one half will survive famine or disease is known to the Barabaig, but it is a topic of controversy that remains unresolved. What is evident is that variation exists in the kinds of residence pat-terns that individual families with large stock-holdings will follow.

Size of the family herd and the carrying capacity of the land are factors that contribute to individual variations in the location of homesteads and in the frequency of moving. Two owners of large herds usually do not care to build their homesteads in the same neighborhood because of the competition for grazing that will almost inevitably ensue. There are no rights to grazing land held either individually or collectively. Anyone may graze his cattle or cultivate, if he is so inclined, wherever he wishes and build his homestead in the vicinity of any clan or lineage member or in-law with whom he wishes to establish closer social re-lations. Therefore, the social composition of a neighborhood changes periodically as neighbors move to other areas and are subsequently replaced by new families. While there is no fixed pattern of social attachment to a particular neighbor-hood, some kinship or in-law relationship is usually the entrée into a new neigh-borhood. At least, in this way, the new social environment will contain some predictable elements.

Foraging

Whether or not a family experiences a food shortage depends to a large extent on the availability of grazing for their cattle. With the advance of the dry season, grass turns brown and becomes close-cropped because of the intensive grazing of numerous herds. When grazing areas become depleted, the animals must walk further each day to obtain the same amount of food. Exhausted from walking long distances to find enough grass to eat, the milch cows are physically unable to maintain normal lactation. During the months of August and September, the milk yield of the cows drops considerably and it is at this time that the Barabaig are faced with food shortage. They can no longer use the dwindling supply of milk they formerly shared with the calves. If the calves are to survive and enlarge the family herd, the available milk of the cows must be reserved for them. Faced with the prospect of losing calves through starvation, a Barabaig herd-owner invariably chooses to find other means of feeding himself and his family. His first thought is to go to his nearest relatives or clansmen for assistance, but in all probability they similarly face a food shortage. Sometimes he is fortunate to be able to borrow a few milch cows from a kinsman whose herd is large enough that they are still producing enough milk for the family. More often, he must organize a search for food, either locally or in neighboring horticultural societies. He may hear that there is maize or millet available in some Somali shops in the trading settlement, but his credit may not be good or the prices may be too high for his meager cash resources. The cattle auction may still be one or two months away. His only remaining solution is to journey to one of the neighboring horticultural tribes and barter for food.

Special equipment and certain information is necessary before setting off to forage. He will need donkeys and grain sacks to carry the maize or millet back to the homestead. If he does not own any donkeys he will have to borrow some from his neighbors or kinsmen. Goats or a young bull will be used as barter in exchange for a number of sacks of cereal grains. With the donkeys, grain pouches, and goats, or bullock, he sets off in a northerly direction to the Iraqw, with whom he feels some friendship and cultural identity. If rumors or first-hand information from friends indicate that the Iraqw are similarly affected by food shortages, he will decide to head in a southerly direction and enter the country of the WaNyaturu, his traditional enemy. If he must barter with his enemies, at least they should not receive one of his young bulls in exchange for their grain. He prefers to trade a goat or two to the WaNyaturu, but if they have had a bad harvest he may have to give them one of his young bulls, which he does only as a last resort.

Having located a WaNyaturu farmer who is willing to barter part of his food surplus, and after a great deal of haggling over price, the Barabaig sets off for home with the donkeys, loaded down with grain sacks, jogging in front of him. He now knows where he can locate food. This information is valuable, and will be divulged only to his closest friends. He expects that they would do the same for him if he were setting out to find food and they had already returned from a successful forage. Sometimes, trade relations with a particular WaNyaturu family may last for a number of years, but more often a Baraband looks for a farmer who is selling grain at the lowest price. In this respect, he strives to minimize losses, whether it is money or cattle.

Cattle Theft

Building up a herd not only entails the acquisition of cattle and skillful herding techniques but it also involves precautions designed to prevent loss of livestock through theft and disease. Since cattle are considered the most valued property, it logically follows that some system of identification of property should exist in Barabaig society. While cattle-stealing among the Barabaig does occur, there are a number of factors that tend to keep the incidence of cattle-theft at a low level. First, it is easier to go to neighboring tribes and steal their mature stock than it is to steal Barabaig cattle and herd these stolen animals in one's own territory. Second, there are so many physical features and behavioral characteristics of Barabaig cattle that lend themselves to easy identification by the owner that cattle-theft is discouraged, although not completely prevented. Only young stock that have not yet been branded are targets of Barabaig cattle-thieves.

Color markings are one of the more obvious means by which herdsmen identify their animals. Animals of a single color—all black, all white, all brown—are more distinguishable than those of mixed color combinations, which constitute the majority of Barabaig cattle. However, unusual color combinations are also easily distinguishable. One highly valued color combination is seen in an animal with a black head, black tail, and a white body. Another desirable color combination exists when an animal has a reddish-brown head, white fore-legs, and black hind-legs. In addition to color, the length and shape of an animal's horns are sometimes used for easy identification. One of the most cherished bulls a man can own is one with one horn pointing forward and one pointing backwards. An owner of such an animal can boast about it during the singing rivalry that takes place as part of the beer-drinks in various Barabaig ritual situations.

Another way in which easy identification of livestock is achieved is through the culturally standardized use of cattle brands. Every bovine animal (that is, cow or bull) carries a set of three distinctive brands on some part of its body. Wealthy cattle owners sometimes apply a fourth brand which identifies the livestock as belonging to a particular family. Otherwise, no family name brands are used. While all cattle are owned and controlled by individual families, the cattle are ultimately the property of a larger social grouping, such as a clan and lineage. Each clan has its own distinctive cattle brand which is burned into the flesh of all cattle born into a family herd. A specific area on the animal's body is reserved for a particular clan. One clan's brand will always be placed on the left side of an animal's neck while another clan will customarily burn its brand into the right rear flanks. Cattle brands, therefore, serve to prevent cattle-theft and aid in identifying the animals on occasions when they are used in various stock transactions which occur during the lifetime of their owners.

Perhaps the most singularly important factor that permits an owner to identify his livestock is the familiarity of behavioral characteristics gained through living with and observing these animals every day. A child growing up in a particular homestead sees his father's and mother's livestock while they are corraled. Later, he accompanies his parent, or his older brother or sister, on daily herding circuits and learns to share herding responsibilities. In close contact with the herd, he gains knowledge about the personal idiosyncracies of each animal. Having spent most of the day with the herd, a herdsman becomes knowledgeable about minute details of his stock. The way a particular bull bellows, or a certain cow walks, is part of the sense-data which is retained in the memory of the herdsman. This was dramatically demonstrated to me on numerous occasions of which I will recount one instance.

During one of my frequent walks, my interpreter-informant and I passed the rim of a large crater at the bottom of which lay a deposit of salt. All the Barabaig herdsmen in the neighborhood periodically brought their herds down into this crater to take advantage of the natural salt lick. On this particular day, a number of herds had already been down and back up. As we walked along peering into the relatively deep crater, my informant stopped and exclaimed, "My wife left one of my cows down there!" I looked down and noticed a tiny shape I could barely make out to be a cow. I asked him how he knew it was his cow. He told me that he was certain it was his cow by the way it tossed its head when it walked. We both went down into the crater and indeed verified that the cow belonged to my informant. I momentarily visualized the domestic scene that might take place when the wife came home with the rest of the herd only to be confronted by the sight of her husband and the stray cow.

Health and Fertility

One of the primary goals of every Barabaig male is to be the owner of a large herd of cattle. Many Barabaig men experience anxiety about the possibility of being poor in cattle—a condition that is subject to gossip and ridicule. In order to insure against the possibility of losing his herd through disease or infertility, a herd-owner will go to a specialist who dispenses "medicine", *madyod*, believed to promote the health and fertility of livestock. For a payment of one female calf, the specialist's fee, the herd-owner receives a powder made from a parasitic plant that grows and thrives on host trees. Upon arriving back to the homestead, the man sprinkles the powder across the entrance gate of the kraal. To make doubly sure that each animal will come in contact with the potion, the "medicine" is also sprinkled across the entrance to the cattle corral and the doorways of the huts housing the young calves, sheep, and goats. The homestead is now considered to be in a state of quarantine for the next two days, the period of effectiveness of the *madyod*. A large forked stick, used for pushing thornbushes in position when building fences, is placed across the gate as a signal to others that the homestead is closed to visitors. Anyone wishing to communicate with members of the family must shout their messages at a distance.

Means of promoting cattle fertility and preventing miscarriage of calves are also available. One does not have to go to a curer. If a particular cow is barren, or has had repeated miscarriages, a strip of skin taken from the hide of a hyena, or an eland, is tied around its neck. The Barabaig believe that both the hyena and eland are animals that experience only normal birth and have offspring which do not die in infancy. Therefore, following a magical principle, the Barabaig conclude that the skins of these animals in contact with the problem cow should transmit the same biological characteristics to the wearer.

Bewitching the Cattle

Death and sickness in cattle requires explanation on some causal basis, and the Barabaig use magical explanations to account for some of the differences between the welfare and condition of one's own herd as compared with herds of other Barabaig. Why should Ganak's herd remain healthy and multiply rapidly while mine is sickly and decimated? What is he doing that I am not doing? Is someone doing something to my animals? Perhaps it is Gidagui with whom I quarreled this morning. These and similar questions are pondered and sometimes openly discussed with friends. If the answers cannot be found in some variable of the physical environment, or in particular herding techniques, then the reasons for misfortune must be sought in the realm of the supernatural.

Most Barabaig men and women carefully avoid gazing upon cattle herds belonging to other families. A man or woman who spends a great deal of time watching other people's cattle will be accused of casting a spell on the herd if one of the animals should suddenly become sick. The gazer is believed to possess an evil eye and must be driven from the neighborhood. A neighbor accused of bewitching cattle may choose to submit to oath in order to proclaim his innocence. However, oath-taking is considered so dangerous that he weighs the consequences of banishment from the community against the dangers of taking an oath. Taking an oath requires a man to place his tongue against the iron blade of a spear and then to pledge that his family, homestead, and cattle be destroyed if he is telling a lie. If he refuses to submit to oath, or fails to leave the neighborhood immediately, a council is convened and a death curse is directed at him. Some of the men construct a litter like the one used to carry out corpses to the bush. Word is circulated that the gazer has died. The men place the litter on top of an ant-hill and run away. Finishing their task, the men wait for the witch to die or go mad within five days. The accused witch usually moves from the neighborhood as soon as he hears that his death litter has been built and taken out into the bush.

Sudden death of any cattle immediately precipitates a crisis situation in the homestead. Knowing well that entire herds have been wiped out by a single animal carrying a disease, a Barabaig herd-owner mobilizes his household into a state of readiness. The dead animal is examined for any outward signs of disease, but no autopsy is performed. If no signs of disease are apparent, the possible cause of death may be narrowed down to an act of sorcery by envious or hostile persons. Perhaps they secretly scattered some evil potion across the gate or under the gate. In this situation of uncertainty, the herd-owner usually decides to use counter-magic to offset or cancel the magical power of the suspected potion. He summons an elder known for his good character and invites him to a beer-drink. A pot of honey-beer is brewed and made ready for the return of the cattle herd. In the evening, when the cows return to the kraal, the elder, sometimes assisted by a young virgin boy of the neighborhood, spray honey beer on the back of each animal as it passes through the gate. After the ritual, the boy returns home while the elder and herd-owner resume their beer-drink. If there are any new deaths in the cattle herd, the family will then move away to another neighborhood.

Economic Gain

Seeking economic gain in cattle is both overtly and covertly practiced, although some livestock transactions contain so many hidden motives and potential trouble areas that economic gain can be easily transformed into economic loss, or worse.

One livestock transaction involving non-kinsmen is an exchange of one type of stock for another because of some specific purpose or goal. When someone needs a bull to use as a sacrificial animal, or for other reasons such as providing meat for a convalescent mother, the owner of a pregnant cow can exchange it for a bull that will then be killed and eaten. The owner of the bull gains temporary custody over the cow and awaits the birth of the calf. He has a legal claim over the calf, which is a counter-payment for the bull the other owner slaughtered. Ideally, the counter-payment should be a female calf that would then be capable of increasing the herd of the new owner. After the weaning of the calf, the mother cow, or dam, is returned to its original owner and the calf remains as counter-payment for the bull. While there are definite rules governing this stock transaction, known as *gefurdyed*, some individuals may deliberately try to exploit the situation to maximize their gain. The case of Dengu is not only illustrative of the institution of *gefurdyed*, but is also a good example of how conflict over livestock leads to the manipulation of both traditional and modern legal systems in attempts to gain economic advantage for one individual and justice for his adversary.

Dengu went to Gilagwend, a member of a rain-making clan, to trade a pregnant cow for an ox. He wished to slaughter it and use its fatty meat to make a soup for his wife, who had just given birth and was convalescing from a difficult delivery. Gilagwend agreed to give Dengu an ox in exchange for a pregnant cow whose calf would become the property of Gilagwend. Some time after the calf was born, Dengu went to Gilagwend's herd to claim his cow. When he arrived to take back his cow, he noticed that the herd was being tended by a young girl. Dengu returned to his kraal with the cow, but without notifying Gilagwend that he had taken it back. For some reason, Gilagwend either forgot about the returned cow or was not notified by the herd-girl. However, the incident was not closed, and later proved to be a source of conflict that was to have serious consequences. After a few years, Dengu noticed that the calf left to Gilagwend as counter-payment in the *gefurdyed* exchange had been a prolific animal, giving birth to calves who also became fertile cows. Dengu also observed that Gilagwend had become senile and was mentally unstable. He decided to take advantage of the situation by claiming that Gilagwend had never returned the cow originally used in the *gefurdyed* transaction and, therefore, he was entitled to all of its progeny. He took his case before a government court (an agency known as the Native Authority) and the court, made up of Barabaig elders paid by funds of the Native Authority, decided to settle the case by requiring the litigants and witnesses to take a traditional oath that would ascertain the guilt or innocence of the parties involved in the dispute. This particular Barabaig oath required each disputant and witness to lick the iron blade of a spear (preferably one owned by a man blinded in one eye) to determine who had lied about the claim. The court adjourned to await results of the spear-licking oath administered to Dengu, Gilagwend, and the woman who had been the herd-girl at the time Dengu had allegedly taken back his cow.

About two weeks after the oath taking, elders of the neighborhood became concerned when the expected rains failed to appear. Elders gathered to accuse Gilagwend, a rain-maker, of holding back the rains. Gilagwend swore his innocence by saying, "If it is my hand, may my home be destroyed." Several days later, Gilagwend's first wife died, and a few days later Gilagwend died. These events were interpreted by the neighborhood council of elders as proof that Gilagwend had lied about withholding the rains. At the same time, the Native Authority court decided that Gilagwend's death was the result of having lied during the spear licking oath. Both groups of Barabaig elders never considered disease or advanced age (both deceased were over 50 years of age) as a possible cause of death. Shortly after, Dengu went to the Native Authority court to claim the 12 head of cattle that Gilagwend had acquired from their original livestock transaction. However, Gilagwend's second wife appealed to the court and the case was finally settled with the awarding of six cattle to Dengu and the remainder going to Gilagwend's survivors.

In the meantime, the drought continued and, with a shortage of grass, the milk yield of cattle was seriously reduced. The Barabaig were faced with a famine situation. Gilagwend's second wife went to the government appointed chief and asked him to administer a different oath to Dengu, which would clear her deceased husband's name and put the blame for the drought on Dengu, who was allegedly responsible for all the misfortune. In taking this oath, Dengu and Gilagwend's second wife would have to lick the blood drawn from the cut ear of one of Dengu's six cows. Dengu was afraid of taking this oath and suggested to the chief that he would give him a calf if the chief would dissuade Gilagwend's wife from insisting on taking the oath. The chief told the woman that the first oath was sufficient proof of Dengu's innocence. The chief tried to collect the calf promised him, but Dengu refused to pay him. Angered at not having received his bribe, the chief gathered a council of tribal elders who then proclaimed that the reason there was a drought was due to Dengu's deception of

Gilagwend and his reluctance to return the rainmaker's cattle back to the rightful heirs. Of the six cows fraudulently obtained from Gilagwend, Dengu had sold three at various cattle auctions to get money to pay for beer-drinks and other expenses. The tribal council imposed a death curse upon Dengu. Dengu has since become a *sid lehat*—a "man without a home." He wanders from place to place, sometimes staying with his nephew or with his married sons. People watch him, expecting him to die from the death curse imposed upon him by the tribal council. He continues to live, although lonely and shunned by everyone except his nearest kin. One day he came to my camp and offered to become my informant, but my fieldwork would have been seriously affected if I had decided to associate with him. Dengu is a tragic figure of a man whose avarice led him to a life of social isolation.

Social Prestige

Every society has its means of affording social prestige to individuals for having exemplified and implemented the highest values of the culture. For the Barabaig, the means for achieving social prestige are both directly and indirectly related to the cattle complex. The struggle for basic biological survival and the struggle for prestige or social recognition takes place in the same arena of life. A Baraband is faced with challenges emanating from both his physical and social environments. Poverty in cattle is a social stigma carrying with it such reference names as "Man without cattle," "Man without a home," and "Man without words." A man whose herd has been depleted or exterminated through disease may be loaned a number of milch cows by his relatives. He herds these animals and uses their milk, and for his labor receives one female calf to begin his own herd again. However, a man who has lost his herd through improvidence and irresponsibility will not be helped by kinsmen and will become an object of ridicule and derision.

To solve the problem of biological survival does not necessarily mean that social survival is assured, although there is a relationship between the two problems. A Baraband who is successful in raising a large herd of cattle is socially recognized as being more knowledgeable and powerful than a person with a small herd. At council meetings, his words will be listened to and deference will be shown him. His reputation precedes him in every neighborhood where his name is a household word. People watch his actions and try to imitate some of his herding techniques in order to capture that elusive variable between success and failure in raising cattle and building up a large herd. They imitate herding whistles and songs sung to a rich man's cattle with the hope of enticing their own animals to greater effort and productivity. Somehow, there must be something he does that they do not do.

Wealth in cattle does not invariably confer prestige to the owner of a large herd unless it is accompanied by other personal attributes. A wealthy man is expected to be generous when relatives come to him for donation of stock. If he is overly generous, his large herd may rapidly become depleted. He usually becomes defensive and secretive concerning the total number and location of his entire stock. However, to gain social recognition from kinsmen, neighbors, and others, he must donate livestock on special ritual occasions, especially those requiring animal sacrifice. By donating an ox for animal sacrifice, he not only gains social prestige but also acquires supernatural benefits from his gift. It is his animal which is offered up to God and the ancestral spirits.

Some rich men are not generous and have gained a reputation for miserliness. They stay much to themselves and are not invited to beer-drinks. While young men may try to marry daughters of these men, the in-law relationships that follow are generally highly sensitive to slight verbal stimuli, but a wife with a large dowry of cattle "closes the mouth of her husband."

Wealthy men with a reputation for generosity are invited to beer-drinks and are usually offered the first drinks from newly brewed beer pots. They are shown deference on numerous occasions, especially from persons whose herds contain animals acquired from wealthy men.

4

Homestead and Household

Settlement Pattern

WITH THE EXCEPTION of a few small trading settlements established by Somali immigrants, there are no villages in Barabaig territory. Individual homesteads are built at a considerable distance from each other—usually more than two hundred yards apart. At no time of the year is there any dense clustering of homesteads around any water supply. Access routes for livestock to enter and leave the crater lakes remain open and unobstructed by any homesteads, although a few homesteads may be located about 300 to 400 yards away from the lakes. From this distance to a seven-mile radius, a number of Barabaig homesteads are scattered at random. Because of the widespread distribution of homesteads, I choose to refer to these settlements as neighborhoods and wards, following Barabaig usage, rather than as villages, for which there is no name in the Barabaig language.

The extent of a neighborhood cannot be delimited solely in terms of physical boundaries, although a certain area can be identified by name. Difficulty in delimitation of a neighborhood stems from the fact that it is not the periphery that is identifiable, but the "center" around which at varying distances a number of homesteads are distributed at random. Therefore, the reference name of the neighborhood derives from some physical landmark, such as a lake, hill, ravine, rock outcrop, or the name of some elder who had received a stone cairn burial.

A Barabaig homestead, *gheid*, consists of a thorn-bush fence 8 to 10 feet in height and built in the shape of a figure-eight, half of which encircles the huts, while the other half serves as a cattle corral, *muhaled*, for the family herd. The living space containing the huts is called a *samod*. There is usually one gate between the two halves. This provides the passage through which people and cattle enter and leave the homestead. Visitors to the homestead are required to call out to get permission before they may pass through the gate or *dosht*. They shout, "People, bring your ears outside!" and then wait for someone to emerge

Homestead with thorn-bush fence in the shape of a figure eight. (Seen from atop a rock outcrop.) Rolling open plains are in the background.

Huts with room sections for six wives of a wealthy cattle-owner.

to recognize them. If no one answers after two or three calls, they leave immediately, lest they be accused of improper behavior. If they are recognized and
invited to enter the homestead, they prop their spears against the fence before
entering the gate; another courtesy and another precaution.

At night, when people and cattle are within the thorn-bush enclosure,
thorn bushes are placed in the entrance to prevent predatory animals (lion,
leopard, wild dog, and hyena) from entering and attacking the livestock or the
people. Night visiting is rare, but occurs during emergencies. Otherwise, people
and cattle are "locked in" for the night.

By looking at certain physical features of a homestead or *gheid* it is possible to estimate the size of a family herd and the social composition of the
household. A Barabaig herd-owner builds a thorn-bush fence to fit the needs of his
cattle and his family. A cattle corral with a small circumference indicates that
the family herd is small in numbers. One hut, or a number of huts, in the living
space, or *samod*, means that the husband has one or more wives. Scarcity of
building materials, conservation of human muscular energy, and lack of personal
pretense, are the factors that prevent a man from building a homestead larger
than is required to adequately house his cattle and family. Besides, every neighbor eventually gets to know many of the details about size of herd and family
from observing the other's homesteads. When neighbors are also relatives, there
is no secrecy about the composition of herd and family belonging to his kinsman.
A stranger to the neighborhood can quickly scan a homestead and arrive at a
good estimate of the wealth and size of the family within. But any prolonged
viewing of a homestead by a stranger might be interpreted as an act of sorcery or
witchcraft.

Variation in the construction of a homestead is related to the availability
of building materials, the size of the cattle herd, and the social composition of
the family. Generally, there is difficulty in finding Y-shaped branches large
enough to serve as uprights for the cross-beams that support the roof, made of
twigs, thatch, mud, and cow-dung. Hut walls are constructed by digging a long
trench into which are placed a number of short, upright poles, which are then
interlaced with long, slender sticks. A mixture of mud and cow-dung is then
applied as a plaster on both sides of the wall. While there are no holes in the
roof to provide ventilation, a number of small holes in the upper part of the
walls serve as vents to let out the smoke from the hut fires. Hut fires burn or
smolder almost continuously and are rekindled when they go out. Unlike some
societies where it is necessary to perform a ritual before a fire can be rekindled,
the Barabaig take no special action to restart a fire, although the ashes of a hearth
are viewed in a magical, mystical way.

Homesteads of monogamous families, that is, families comprising one
husband and one wife, are small in size, often with one hut divided into two
compartments—the husband's room, called *huland*, and the *ged*, or wife's room.
Sometimes there is a third section, called *dododa muhog*, a place where sheep,
goats, and young calves are kept. Each person's room has its own hearth, but
the fire in the husband's room is merely for heating purposes and is rarely used
for cooking. A wife cooks for her husband in her own room and then brings the

food to him in the *huland*. The hearth in her room has a special magical significance, which is associated with the cooking stones and the ashes. A hearth consists of three large stones placed on the ground in the form of a triangle. These stones support the cooking pots and partially enclose the wood fires. On her wedding day the wife brings these stones into her husband's homestead and they will remain in the same position until the family moves away, in which case they will be carried along and placed in the new homestead. The left and right stones symbolize the wife and husband, respectively, while the stone at the apex of the triangle represents the children. Upon death of a member of the family, the appropriate stone will be thrown away, but only in the death of children will the appropriate stone be replaced. Death of a husband or wife closes the hearth and creates a situation which the Barabaig refer to as "cold room."

Homesteads of polygynists differ in size and complexity from those built by a husband and wife. A polygynous household consists of a husband, two or more wives, and their children. Barabaig men strive for an ideal situation in which they acquire many cows, many wives, and many children. While many husbands have two or three wives, some men have as many as eight wives, but generally no more than four wives occupy a homestead. By splitting up the family and their herds and building two separate homesteads at some distance from each other, a Barabaig husband believes that he reduces possible conflict between the wives and ensures the survival of at least part of his cattle herd by "spreading the risk."

When a woman marries, she is required to leave her family homestead and go to live either in the homestead of her father-in-law, if it is the first marriage for her husband, or she must occupy quarters in her husband's homestead if he already has one or more wives and is living in separate residence away from his father. Each new wife added to a polygynous household occupies living quarters furthest away from the homestead gate. Although her room or hut is at the end of a line of huts, she is generally not at the end of the line in the affections of her husband.

The men's hut, *huland*, is always built nearest the gate and its doorway always faces toward the gate in order to permit surveillance of the entrance. A gateway is a passage for the family and their herd, but it is also a source of danger, a weak spot in the defenses of the homestead. The *huland* is occupied by the head of the household, referred to as *gwargwed* (an honorific term also denoting a respected elder), his unmarried sons, and, on occasion, by male visitors. The interior contains a place for a fire and a low bed or platform made of poles over which a number of stiff cow skins are thrown. Some gourds and a spear or two complete the furnishings. Since Barabaig herd-owners must move their homesteads periodically in order to find grazing areas for their cattle, a minimum of material objects and possessions is both practical and desirable.

Depending on personal preference or the availability of building materials, the first wife may have her own hut next to the *huland* or a separate room in her husband's hut. A woman's room is shared by her daughters and by those sons who are six years of age or under and who are considered to be too young to be included in the group of brothers sharing the *huland* with their father. Since

Barabaig males spend most of their waking day outside the homestead, shared sleeping quarters neither promote nor adversely affect a spirit of unity among brothers. Personal friendships between brothers develop by chance rather than emerge as a result of having the same or different mother.

Sharing a Homestead and Husband

Each room-group or hut-group is a separate domestic unit with its own livestock holdings and its own sphere of rights and duties. Each mother normally cooks for her husband and her own children. Preparing and serving food to her husband may be done in turns by different co-wives. A harmonious household is one in which wives share the duties of cooking for their husband. Some polygynous households are torn apart by dissent, distrust, and gnawing fear. In these households, the husband is careful to avoid provoking heated arguments between his wives, but his actions, even though guarded, may result in a domestic flare-up. Wives in disharmonious households cook separate meals for their husband each day. He must be careful to eat the same amount of food from each wife's bowl. If he eats more from one bowl than from another, when the women return to their huts, there may be rounds of angry accusations of sorcery hurled between the wives. "Why did he eat more out of your bowl than he did out of mine?" "What did you put in your food?" Many a night air is filled with the sounds of angry wives accusing each other of evil intentions while the husband sits in his hut "like a lion in a den."

Although wives are ranked in order of their marriage, the first wife exercises only nominal authority over her co-wives, the co-wife relationship being, for the most part, of an egalitarian character. Friendship and cooperation among co-wives is based on personal preference, although rank order in terms of seniority and juniority does play a part in determining which wives will be friends and associates. Generally speaking, in a family of four or more wives, the first wife and second wife will not be associates, but will choose lesser wives as their helpmates and confidantes. Whether or not the domestic relations between co-wives and their children are harmonious depends upon a number of factors, not the least of which is the husband's diplomacy, intelligence, and ability to divide his attention and favors equally among his wives and to wield authority when disputes threaten to erupt into physical violence. For the Barabaig, a good homestead or "gheidami" is a quiet one with the soft, musical laughter of women and the happy play of children.

Herding duties are usually shared by co-wives and their older children. Although each hut-group owns and controls its own livestock, the various stock of the family segments are merged and tended as a single herd. However, in the morning and evening, each wife will milk only those cows belonging to her or allocated as milch cows by her husband. If a wife is sick, her husband may help with the milking chores; but if there are co-wives with whom she is friendly, her confidante will milk her cows and feed her children.

Family and Clan

Within a polygynous family, each wife and her children comprise a discrete, social unit with social position in the family hierarchy determined by the order of marriage of the wife. Children derive their status according to the rank of their mother, their own order of birth, and their sex. Children of one mother identify their full blood relationship by the term *giyanya* in order to differentiate themselves from children of their father's other wives, *ghahanya*, who form their own distinct groupings.

Every person born into Barabaig society automatically becomes a member of a number of different groups. He is a member of a family and, at the same time, acquires membership in a larger social grouping called a clan. A clan or *dosht* (gate) as it is referred to by the Barabaig, is the largest social grouping composed of male and female members who claim common descent from some founding ancestor in the distant past whose family constituted the original group. Membership in a clan is automatically conferred by birth, depending upon which parent is considered the culturally appropriate one through whom descent is traced. Descent is mainly concerned with defining social relationships between people who are descendants of some common ancestor. These social relationships are governed by sets of rights and obligations that are binding for the lifetime of an individual and may extend to his children as well. There is nothing a person can do about changing his clan membership, but there is an opportunity provided by marriage in which nominal or provisional membership in a spouse's clan is granted. If a person wishes to remain within Barabaig society, he must be located in time and space as a member of a clan. One does not repudiate clan membership, with its concomitant rights and duties, and yet remain an acceptable member of Barabaig society.

Barabaig clans are patrilineal, which is to say that they determine membership by tracing descent or, more appropriately, ascent, through a long line of male connecting links starting with the father and up to the father's father, to the father's father's father and so forth until the founding father is reached. Tracing descent requires memorization and retention of personal names of all male connecting links up to the ancestor of the clan. Actually, memory fails the Barabaig when they reach about ten generations back from their own. Distortion occurs in the order and existence of those male descendants closest to the founding ancestor. Membership in a clan is membership in a "mutual-aid society" in which members are obligated to render social, economic, and political assistance to clansmen in trouble.

Extended Household

Households expand and contract as sons marry and later move away. Formation of a social grouping larger than the polygynous family takes place when the oldest son brings his future wife to live in his father's homestead. The addition of a daughter-in-law to a family results in an extended household. If the husband-to-be is the first son of the first wife, a special hut for the betrothed girl is built in the cattle corral, *muhaled*, the only instance when a hut is built inside the corral. Barabaig say that an intended bride living in the corral is given the opportunity to view and learn to recognize on sight the livestock her husband will inherit from his father and mother. The girl continues to live in the cattle corral for a variable period of from three days to two months, depending upon completion of wedding and marriage arrangements and the consummation of marriage. A new hut is then built for her at the end of the line of huts occupied by her father-in-law's wives. Her husband continues to share the *huland* with his father. After an indeterminate period, usually not exceeding one year, the son asks permission of his father to move away and establish a separate homestead, either nearby or in a different neighborhood. While the father may resent the impending autonomy of his son because he loses a productive worker as well as part of the family herd, he nevertheless realizes that he has no legal grounds on which to refuse permission unless he becomes an invalid. A request by the eldest son for permission to move away from the homestead also brings to the father the realization that he is advancing in years and that his parental authority is threatened. As a patriarch, he is responsible for the behavior of any male member of the household in relation to the neighborhood group, lineage, clan, and tribe. His obligations toward his family include the payment of bride-wealth when his sons marry, dowry when his daughters marry, and payment of any fines levied against his sons or daughters for any offense they may commit outside the homestead. He is not legally responsible for any of his wife's actions with regard to outside social relations. Fathers are forever legally liable for their daughters' offenses, since women are considered legal minors whose illegal actions and culpability are the responsibility of their fathers rather than their husbands. Establishment of an autonomous homestead and household away from the father is one of the ideals which Barabaig men seek and eventually accomplish. Once a man moves his family and cattle herd out of his father's homestead, he assumes legal responsibility over his own affairs.

If hostility exists between father and son, the son will build his own *huland* on the opposite side of the *samod*. His wife's hut will be located next to it during the early period of the marriage. If the son asks his father for permission to establish a new homestead and the father refuses (which sometimes happens) the son may subvert his authority by secretly moving his wife and their cattle to a new location. He may even bring his own mother with him if she is one of the father's lesser wives. The secret flight of mother, son, daughter-in-law, and livestock may arise from strained domestic relations between father and son or husband and wife. Secret flight of mother and son is only possible when there are no other children in the hut-group. No divorce proceedings are initiated by either husband or wife, and the woman continues to live in her married son's homestead without marrying again. Neither are any cattle formerly allocated to the woman by her husband returnable to him.

The birth of a son to the wife irrevocably ends any return of marriage cattle, either because of a wife's separation, divorce, or death. However, the patriarch customarily initiates legal action against his married son. Not only does the son's act of secession with mother and cattle constitute a breach in domestic relations, but it is viewed as a violation of certain domestic rights that the father holds over the son's mother by virtue of the bridewealth payment that initially established the marriage bond and conferred on the husband the rights over the domestic labor of his wife. Secession of a married son and his mother is therefore an offense committed against the father and punishable by a cattle fine. The fine, *ghordyod baland,* or "fine of the son," levied by the father against his son customarily consists of one bull and one cow with calf, and indicates that despite the shift in residence the father still exercises a degree of authority over his son. The son invariably pays the fine because he fears spirit vengeance in later years when his father dies.

Composition of the Family Herd

The complexity of property relations among the Barabaig is visually apparent in the composition of the family herd. Within a particular homestead, rights in livestock derive from different principles and sources. A family herd is composed of animals originating from different social and ritual situations and from different donors. The mixed assortment of cattle displaying different cattle brands is graphic evidence of the multi-faceted property complex of the Barabaig. While each animal carries three different brands—the father's clan, mother's clan, and the father's mother's clan—a large number of animals within the family herd may not share the same brands, although they belong to the same owner.

Ownership of cattle is the prerogative of males in Barabaig society, but the position of women in the network of stock relations is crucial. Although a woman cannot own cattle outright, she does exercise some control over stock given to her as gifts on ritual occasions, and can be considered as a kind of temporary holding-unit from which in-payments of stock will eventually become out-payments to her children as they mature, marry, and later move away to establish families and homesteads of their own.

Each hut-group, composed of a mother and her children within a polygynous household, is an autonomous property-owning unit. The size of a herd which a particular hut-group owns and controls depends on a number of factors, such as size of the mother's dowry, amount of marriage cattle given to the mother by her husband and relatives, and the number of animals solicited for her sons on the occasion of their first-teeth eruption. (All of these stock transfers will be discussed in subsequent sections.) The amount of livestock a wife brings to a marriage in the form of dowry varies according to the wealth in cattle of her family, lineage, and clan. Therefore, since a man may have wives belonging to different clans, the size of each hut-group's livestock holdings may vary. The first wife and her children may not own and control as many head of cattle as a lesser co-wife. Nevertheless, all of the animals belonging to the husband, his wives, and their children are herded together and corraled as a single family herd. Only during milking time will certain cows be separated from the general herd and milked by their female owners. Otherwise, any separation of the family herd is done in the minds of the owners.

A husband cannot sell any of his wife's dowry cattle unless she is consulted. Once a wife has given birth to a son, her control over her dowry is weakened by the fact that ownership rights of the donors have now been transferred over to her son. If the husband's stock holding is smaller than that of a wife, he tends not to be argumentative towards his wife because, as the Barabaig explain, the presence of a large dowry "closes the mouth" of the husband. The existence of dowry gives a woman economic "leverage" in her relations vis-à-vis the husband, which diminishes somewhat with the birth of a son but increases again when the son reaches the age at which he and his mother could separate from the father's household and set up a separate homestead in a different neighborhood. While the son is very young, the father may sell some of his wife's dowry cattle or use the cattle for his own personal advantage in a livestock transaction. Marital relations become strained when the wife, guardian of her sons' and daughters' livestock, objects to the dissipation of her dowry stock by her husband. As her eldest son reaches the age of understanding and realizes what is happening to his mother's cattle, he sides with his mother. Then a bitter rivalry may break out between the son and the father. A woman's dowry cattle are not only a source of food and economic support to a household, but may also provide the main stimulus for quarrels and dissensions.

A mother's dowry cattle eventually become the property of her sons and daughters; daughters receive their dowry from their mother's dowry and sons receive first-teeth cattle and marriage cattle and inherit the remainder of her stock. However, when a woman lives past the age of childbearing, out-payments of stock to her sons and daughters have depleted most of her herd so that there are only relatively few animals remaining in her herd by the time she nears the end of her life cycle.

The first son of each wife is in an economically advantageous position with regard to the use and inheritance of his mother's dowry cattle. When his mother dies, the first son is morally obligated to distribute some of his mother's dowry stock to his younger full brothers. He will also acquire the moral responsibility of donating dowry cattle to his sisters when they marry. If he chooses not to contribute stock to his brothers and sisters, which does not often occur, there is no legal recourse available to his brothers and sisters to force him to donate animals, but a lasting animosity results from his avariciousness. In a society in which the vagaries of the physical environment affect the growth and depletion of cattle herds, the principle of reciprocity is a means of "spreading the risk." Gifts of livestock to brothers and sisters can be redeemable at a later date. Therefore, to act morally in distributing a mother's dowry cattle is not difficult when faced with possible stock loss through disease or famine.

Division of Meat

Whenever a cow or bull dies of disease or old age, the animal is cooked and eaten by members of the household. No animal is deliberately killed for its meat, with the exception of goats, which are considered a source of meat. Not every family herd includes a flock of goats or sheep, although their numbers have been rising for some time. The rise in numbers of families keeping goats and sheep may be an indication of a greater need to rely upon a more predictable source of food. The Barabaig do not view their cattle as a living supply of beef, but if an animal dies of natural (or unnatural) causes they do not hesitate to use the meat. Anyone who would kill a cow or bull just for food would be the object of intense ridicule and derision if his deed were discovered and made known.

Animals killed during a ritual occasion are considered to be in a special category and the division of meat is determined by a culturally prescribed set of rules. Each portion of meat has its own distinct name, and distribution of certain parts to relatives follows lines according to the social relationship existing between the owner of the animal and the prescribed recipient.

Black oxen are generally used as sacrificial animals during a number of major rituals (such as funerals) performed by the Barabaig. The hump, *hukt*, of an ox is a fatty portion reserved for and sent to the father of the owner of the ox. If the father is not alive, the *hukt* is sent to his eldest surviving brother or to an elder holding senior rank in the father's clan. Other portions of the sacrificial animal, such as the neck, rump, and stomach lining, are sent to the father-in-law, mother's brother, and mother's sister's daughter, respectively. Distribution of meat is considered both a moral and legal obligation, the latter backed by a punitive sanction in the form of a cattle fine imposed by the prescribed male recipient of the meat in the event that he does not receive his rightful share.

Visit of Ancestral Spirits

When a person dies, it is believed that his spirit leaves the body and journeys to the nether world, *utaŋanyid* where he meets his relatives, friends, and all the cattle that had died in his lifetime. Things are almost the same in this place under the ground as they are above with certain outstanding exceptions. Grass is lush, green, and abundant, each cow is full of milk, and there is no disease or death.

Barabaig believe that certain ancestral spirits can visit the homesteads of living relatives in the form of a snake. Snakes are numerous in Barabaig territory and are of poisonous and nonpoisonous variety. Poisonous snakes most commonly encountered are the cobra, puff adder, black and green mambas, and various vipers. There is a wide assortment of nonpoisonous snakes of which the python is the most mysterious but least frequently seen. One small, nonpoisonous black snake is especially significant for the Barabaig who do not consider it a snake at all, but merely an ancestral spirit in the outward form of a snake. Only the spirits of dead members of priestly or ritual clans, *daremgadyeg*, are believed capable of returning from the nether world to visit relatives.

Appearance of a small black snake within a homestead is an occasion for concern and speculation about reasons for the visit. If the snake is seen in the homestead of a member of a nonpriestly or lay clan, *homat'k*, it is interpreted as an evil omen. The homestead-owner suspects that someone has sent the snake to strangle him in his sleep. Perhaps, it is someone with whom he recently had a violent quarrel or fight, or someone to whom he failed to send cows when demanded. If his anxiety and fear of sorcery is strong enough, he may go to a priest or ritual specialist. In return for a magical anointment and assurance that the snake will disappear and not revisit the homestead, the home-owner pays a fee of one female calf to the ritual specialist. It is a ritual solution to anxiety which depletes the herd of one man and at the same time increases the herd of another.

Visits of the small black snake, called *ichibod buŋed*, or "snake of the funeral," is interpreted differently by a member of a priestly or ritual clan. Appearance of a snake in the home of a *daremgadyand* or ritual specialist is a sign that something is wrong in the household. Perhaps one of the wives has been committing repeated acts of adultery. He calls all of his wives together and confronts them with the evidence. He tells them that he has tried to feed the snake with some butter placed at the end of a stick, but that the snake refuses to eat. The snake does not go away, but continues to roam about the homestead. He questions them further about their activities. "Why is this snake here?" "What are you doing that he dislikes?" If one of the wives confesses, sometimes after being accused by an unfriendly co-wife, the errant wife may be beaten or, if she is habitually adulterous, she may be divorced. The husband then brews some honey-beer and pours an offering on the ground near the huts, saying, "Here is your beer, Father (or grandfather)". "Watch my house." "Don't hide anything if you see something wrong." He looks around the kraal for the black snake, but it has long since disappeared.

5

Getting a Start in Life

The Prevalence of Disease

I T IS AN OBVIOUS FACT that a society can survive only if it devises certain solutions for the replacement of personnel lost to it by reason of emigration or death. While motivation in individuals to reproduce themselves is taken care of by psycho-biological drives of a sexual nature, a society must also find adequate solutions to problems of sterility, fertility, miscarriage, infant mortality, and deaths in children and adults. Among the Barabaig, replacing societal members is a question of being able to have children and to keep alive those that are born. Population fluctuations affect the kinds of ecological adjustment possible, given the cultural repertory, and the social and physical environments.

Birth rate among the Barabaig is limited by biological and cultural conditions. The presence of a wide variety of disease-causing organisms in the physical environment imposes certain problems on the Barabaig that may or may not be amenable to cultural solutions, depending upon the magnitude of the problem and people's knowledge and ability to recognize a problem when it exists.

Sterility and miscarriage are two problems that many Barabaig women must face before motherhood becomes a reality for them. While there are many causes for sterility in women, a high incidence of venereal disease among Barabaig women is probably responsible for the tubal obstructions that prevent conception. Traditionally, problems of sterility in women and men (when recognized and conceded) are treated by resorting to ritual solutions.

Many women who become pregnant subsequently have miscarriages. Two major environmental factors—the presence of malaria mosquitoes and contaminated water supplies—contribute to a high incidence of miscarriages. During the rainy season, attacks of malaria are frequent and severe enough to bring about many miscarriages. Domestic use of stagnant lake water during the dry season causes dysentery, which seriously affects a woman's chances of retaining her fetus. Thus, a number of disease-causing organisms are responsible for keeping a check on birth rate and consequently on population growth among the Barabaig.

The characteristic pattern of short life-span so evident in many of the so-called developing areas of the world is strikingly present in Barabaig society.

Few elders reach 50 years of age, and those who do are accorded special consideration and deference. While constant exposure to certain pathogens, such as malarial parasites, may lead to accommodation and tolerance, other disease-causing organisms are so virulent as to preclude the possibility of developing an immunity to the disease. Periodically, a fulminating type of meningitis strikes down young and old alike. Epidemics of whooping cough kill off hundreds of Barabaig children and debilitated adults. Those weakened by other diseases succumb to pneumonia.

Diseases associated with the keeping of cattle are also prevalent and responsible for many deaths. Living in close association with cattle, the Barabaig contract a wide variety of diseases, most of which prove fatal. Tuberculosis in cattle is transmitted to man, and Barabaig infect Barabaig. Both the bovine and human types of tuberculosis are present. Cattle hides carry the spores of the anthrax bacillus, which can also live on top of the soil for a period of more than 15 years. Dust clouds stirred up by walking cattle perpetuate the infection-reinfection cycle. Almost 100 percent of individuals with anthrax die of the disease within three days.

Not all diseases contracted through association with cattle are as fatal to the Barabaig as tuberculosis and anthrax. Relapsing fever, a disease caused by spirochetes transmitted by cattle ticks, has a low mortality rate, but is higher in young children and in persons whose weakened physical condition predisposes them to pneumonia (usually the ultimate cause of death). The practice of keeping young livestock in sections of the huts contributes to the high incidence of relapsing fever. At night, ticks leave the bodies of the young stock and bite the sleeping people. Ticks also infest the huts and may be picked up when walking through tall grass. Although the Barabaig inspect their bodies for burrowing ticks, there are no permanent preventive measures against this ever-present pest. Cattle dips have been built near cattle marketplaces by the veterinarian department of the government. Periodically, whole herds are sent through the dips, which clear the cattle of lice and ticks but re-infestation occurs after the chemical coating loses its potency. Thus, even the intervention of Western veterinary medicine only temporarily affects the ecological balance between the Barabaig, their cattle, and their physical environment. A Barabaig child is born into a disease-ridden environment.

Perils of Pregnancy

When a woman discovers that she is pregnant, she reacts with mixed emotions. The period of pregnancy and the birth event are viewed with apprehension and fear. Barabaig linguistic usage refers to a pregnant woman and an enemy in the same terms. A pregnant woman is "one with enemy" because the fetus she carries within her is her enemy and can cause her death.

Pregnancy brings with it a number of avoidances to be observed by the expectant mother and the household. No one is allowed to use a pregnant woman's drinking and cooking utensils. It is believed that should someone else use them, they would ingest intestinal worms from her fetus. Her pregnancy does not curtail her water-carrying and herding duties until her pregnancy is well along into the final months. However, she must be especially careful while herding cattle so as not to look at any passing wart-hogs, lest her child be born with large tusks for teeth and a bumpy skin. Like produces like.

When labor pains are first felt by the wife, her husband selects a female elder from among the women of the neighborhood to act as midwife. Most middle-aged women have witnessed and assisted in many deliveries, although some women are more proficient than others in diagnosing certain symptoms of labor and in performing duties associated with midwifery. The husband and other men are not permitted to witness a childbirth and are subject to a cattle fine levied by a neighborhood council of women in the event that they either deliberately or accidentally see a woman giving birth.

Delivery is performed in a sitting position on a cow-skin, a small mound of cow-dung, or on an overturned wooden trough. There are no precautions taken against possible infection during delivery with the exception of a taboo against the insertion of hands into the birth canal to guide the passage of the baby. Two methods are used to correct a prolonged delivery. A leather thong is fastened and unfastened around the mother's stomach to apply a downward pressure on the womb. A second method is to seat the woman about 2 feet from the fire. It is believed that the fire will "warm the blood" of the mother and speed up the delivery. As the baby emerges, it is caught by the midwife and placed near the mother while the umbilical cord is cut and tied with sinew. The navel cord is left about two inches long, and after a few days, when it falls off, it is placed between the toes of a young calf as a fertility charm. It eventually gets lost somewhere around the homestead.

After delivery, the midwife winds a long leather strap around the stomach of the new mother. It is worn for two or three days, and its purpose is to dispel any of the fetal sac that might still be lodged inside the mother. The midwife attends the new mother for about ten days, and is then paid one goat-skin and some tobacco, the traditional fee of a midwife.

Although many deliveries proceed without complication, there are some that result in death to the mother and child. If the baby has twisted in the course of its descent in the birth canal and is lodged in a position from which it cannot free itself, the child will be left inside and the mother will be left to hemorrhage and die. Sometimes, a midwife will violate the birth taboo and reach inside to help pull out the baby. This action generally leads to infection (puerperal sepsis) and the mother dies within a few days. Childbearing is one of the major occupational hazards of Barabaig women and is responsible for many deaths in the fertile female upon whom the society relies for its future members.

Infancy and Survival

Certain value attitudes about cow's milk and milk products are fostered by the kind of symbiotic relationship that exists between the Barabaig and their cattle. Each depend upon the other for their biological existence. Since the Barabaig traditionally rely upon their cattle as their main source of food, it is logical that they should have developed strong attitudes about the value of milk and its by-products. Milk is the staple food of the Barabaig and is sometimes converted into butter, which is believed to be sacred and is used on special occasions as a ritual anointment.

A new-born child is fed raw cow's milk during the first three days of its life. The milk is held in the unwashed, cupped hand of the mother. The rationale behind this childrearing practice is two-fold—it serves to introduce the child, at birth, to the traditional food it will rely upon for the rest of its life, and it prevents the child from ingesting the colostrum (the initial watery substance of the mother's breast milk), which is believed to be dangerous for the child. Raw cow's milk is considered ideal and the only "appropriate" food to give an infant a "good start" in a pastoral society. Most infants develop severe diarrhea as a result of this practice, and many die during their first few weeks of life. Apparently, the highly valued cow's milk is never suspected of being the causal agent of death. Those children who survive this childrearing practice barely replace the members of the tribe who die from other causes. In fact, in order to replace deceased members it was necessary to develop the institution of sale and adoption of children from neighboring tribes. In pre-colonial times, children were bought from indigent parents living in adjacent tribal areas. Erroneous belief that the initial breast milk of the mother is dangerous, and the faulty solution of feeding raw cow's milk to a new-born infant drastically reduce an infant's chances of surviving its early weeks of life. Thus, an inadequate solution to the problem of feeding a new-born child creates additional problems of a greater severity and consequence for the child and society.

Having survived the trauma of birth and the cultural hazards of early infancy, a Barabaig infant has still to face a number of situations and living conditions that will affect his chances of living long enough to become an adult. Exposure to various diseases, such as hookworm, ringworm, and other parasites, will keep him debilitated and weakened throughout his lifetime. He will never experience the sensation of good health.

Birth and Death

News of a birth spreads throughout a neighborhood as quickly as news of other importance. After waiting two days or so to determine whether the infant is still alive, the neighborhood women approach the homestead to assist in various activities. A male goat is selected from the family herd and is strangled and butchered by the women. If there are no goats in the homestead, a goat from a neighbor's flock is either solicited or taken without permission. Any objections on the part of a male owner of a goat will be countered with a threat by the women to bring the man before a women's court for failure to render assistance to a new mother. Soup is made from the goat and is fed to the mother, while other portions of the goat are distributed to the women. The midwife has the right to claim the goat-skin as part of her "fee."

A mission of sympathy, *werwerik*, for the new mother is organized by women neighbors. Gifts of milk and maize flour are brought to her homestead and in return the women receive gifts of butter and maize porridge, which they consume at the homestead. Dancing and singing of lewd songs by visiting women continue for a number of days while the new mother remains out of sight. Only her close female relatives will be permitted to see her or her new baby. After a few days, the gift-giving, dancing, and singing come to an end and quiet returns to the neighborhood.

During the one-month convalescence period, it may become necessary for the mother to break her isolation if her baby's health rapidly grows worse. In an emergency, a mother may take her baby away from the homestead to seek medical assistance from a government or mission dispensary or hospital, these facilities being of recent construction. She is careful to avoid all women whom she may encounter while outside the kraal. The child is carried in a soft cradle or sling pressed skin-to-skin against the mother's back. If she meets a woman along a path, the mother throws her cape over her head and crouches to the ground. By her action she tries to convey the impression that "she is not there," and therefore the woman should not speak to her. The outside world is a place full of danger for her and her child. Her isolation and self-imposed silence end when her month-long convalescence is over. She returns to the normal activities of the homestead and neighborhood when the danger period has passed, but she never fully relaxes her vigil over the infant. She knows that children die easily and fast. Her husband is not allowed to resume sexual relations with her for a period of approximately one year, or until the child has learned to walk.

If a child dies, the mother must face another period of isolation or social taboo for yet another month. Death occurring inside a homestead imposes a social stigma on the entire family because death pollutes. A situation of uncleanliness exists no matter what the age or sex of the deceased person might be. However, the death of a child up to the age of three years requires certain ritual precautions. In mourning, the mother shaves her head and reverses her skin garments. She must clean out the ashes from her hearth fire and throw away the cooking stone that represented her child. Her hut is disassembled and rebuilt outside the kraal fence, where she will live in isolation for a period of up to six months. She is allowed to cook for her children, if there are any, but her co-wives and children avoid her because they fear that she might contaminate them with her breast milk. It is believed that any contact with milk from her still-dripping breasts will bring death to children. Her husband no longer receives invitations from his male friends to drink and eat with them. While it is safe to talk with him, his personal possessions, such as tobacco, clothing, stick, and spear are carefully avoided. No one visits or helps around his kraal. After a six-month residence in her isolation hut, the mother throws away her old skirt and makes a new one. Replacement of a fertility panel, made from the skin of a sacrificed sheep and sewn in the front of her leather skirt, is necessary before she is allowed to rejoin her co-wives within the kraal.

When death of a person over three years of age occurs in a family, everyone in the neighborhood must be alerted to the fact that a threat has entered the area. One of the women of the family goes outside the kraal fence and begins to wail, and this summons neighbors to the homestead. One of the requisites of being a good neighbor is to participate in mourning rites. Men gather in groups to discuss the circumstances surrounding the death, while the women continue to wail. Two men are sent to guard the body, while others prepare a litter upon which the corpse will be carried eastward from the homestead and placed in an open spot where it will be consumed by hyena. Most men and women and all children are destined for the belly of the hyena. Only influential male elders and some prominent women are given burials—a special mark of social distinction.

Having wailed long enough to summon all of the women in the neighborhood, some of the women of the family enter their huts to remove all of the skin beds, gourds, pots, food, and other articles and place these outside the fence. The men's council continues to deliberate about brewing honey-beer to take away the curse of death. A woman from the neighborhood must also be selected to clean out ashes from the hearth. She must be a widow without small children. If the deceased is a young boy or girl, the mother will clean her own room. But the death of an adult requires the services of an elderly woman. Some women, upon hearing that they have been selected to clean the room of the deceased, avoid the unpleasant and potentially dangerous task by running away. They go to visit a relative for a few days until the crisis in the neighborhood is over.

After the corpse has been laid out in the bush for the hyena and the room and hearth ashes have been swept clean, all of the household articles are returned to the rooms. The men busy themselves brewing large pots of honey-beer that will be consumed as ritual potions to end the state of pollution existing within the homestead. Some of the honey-beer and its residue may be sprayed around the kraal, especially near the huts, cattle corral, and gate, as an extra added precaution against the return of death. If another death occurs in the household, the family abandons the homestead and moves to another neighborhood where it is believed the family and their cattle will remain healthy and multiply.

Early Training

For the first year of its life, a Barabaig infant is carried around in a leather sling strapped to the back of its mother. There it enjoys the warm comfort of skin-to-skin contact with her. As long as the infant is not yet ready to walk, the mother carries it around wherever she goes. From a fig tree, considered to be sacred because it is associated with God, some bark is stripped and fashioned into a necklace or girdle as a protective charm to ward off disease from the child. Since God sits on a fig tree at the eastern horizon, earthly fig trees similarly possess supernatural power. The infant accompanies its mother on her daily domestic rounds and is given the breast to suckle whenever it cries. While the mother kneels in back of a tilted slab of stone and grinds maize kernels with downward strokes of a long round stone, the child on her back is rocked to sleep by the grinding motion of the mother. Whenever a baby cries and is not appeased by being offered the breast to suckle, the mother will simulate her maize-grinding motions. She bends her body at the waist, backwards and forwards, and makes grinding sounds with her mouth. If it is late at night, the mother may resort to threats to quiet a crying child. A mother may say, "Quiet, or I'll throw you to the hyena." or "Hyena, come and carry away the one who is crying." From the tone of the mother's voice and the sounds of hyena laughing in the darkness a child soon learns to control its crying. Indeed, the childhood experience is so vivid and memorable that adult Barabaig fear darkness and the hyena. Yet, these individuals are the same persons who willingly set out to hunt the lion, elephant, rhino, and cape buffalo armed only with a spear. Women do not venture out after dark, but some men may under special circumstances journey from one place to another. To keep up their spirits and to notify people of their presence while walking past their kraals, men sing special kill-songs, *ranginod*, which may also be sung to discourage any carnivores in the vicinity.

Some mothers who do not like children let them cry, and only occasionally attempt to pacify them. Children of apathetic mothers appear to grow up with feelings of rejection and may habitually go to sleep with another mother and her children. Indeed, a rejected child may spend more time with a mother substitute than with its own mother. Fathers generally spend little time with their children, preferring to sit in the men's hut with male friends. Indulgent mothers pamper their children and spend time teaching them songs and telling them stories. Some mothers while singing admonish their sons by telling them that they should not be lazy or cowardly like sons of other clans. In this way, mothers contribute to the intense rivalry between clans by fostering a sense of competition and clan honor in their young sons.

Mothers control their children by verbal threats rather than corporal punishment. If a boy misbehaves, his mother may threaten to cut off his penis and give it to his sister or to the hyena. He will go crying to his father, who will reassure him that it will not happen. He returns to his mother to tell her what his father said.

Weaning takes place when a child reaches about two years of age. A child will be weaned earlier if it continues to bite its mother's nipples even when slapped across the thighs. At night, the child is sent to sleep with a co-wife of the mother for approximately two weeks, during which time it may try to get milk from the breast of the mother substitute but, failing in this, the child soon gives up in its attempts to suckle.

Naming of a child does not follow any set pattern, but is the result of a slow, casual process in which numerous names are given until one or two names emerge as permanent ones. Many of the earlier names, related to some event during childbirth or shortly after, may persist throughout the period of name selection. "House of sorrow" is a name usually given to a child born at a time when the homestead was in mourning. "Near the lake" and "Outside the kraal" are names referring to the birth event taking place before the mother could get back to the homestead. "Bad legs," "Bad cough," and "Dysentery" are descriptive terms of the child's physical condition. When a name gains common usage in the household, it remains for the lifetime of the individual.

When a child begins to walk, he is usually given to an older sister or to a neighbor's girl to tend. When a toddler gets tired of walking, it is carried around on the hip of an older child. Crawling behavior in children is actively discouraged.

Children are reared in an environment that brings them into close contact with the animal life around them. As they toddle, walk, and tumble about the kraal, they develop a sense of oneness with the young calves, goats, and sheep that inhabit the living space around the huts. Piles of animal dung litter the cattle corral and living space attracting swarms of flies that rest upon man and beast alike. Flies feeding on the moisture of a person's eyes are usually not chased away with hand motions. A tolerance of flies is developed to the extent that a fly can alight on a person's eye without causing him to blink. They are an ever present part of the physical environment to which the Barabaig must adjust. Flies, together with dusty gale force winds and smokey fires, are major contributing factors of chronic eye disorders in young and old alike. Blindness occurs among people of all ages and may be due to venereal infection, disease-carrying flies or mechanical abrasion and trauma. Blind children remain within the homestead and rarely venture outside the kraal unaccompanied. Their world is restricted to the confines of the kraal and a small area outside the gate.

"Cattle of the Tooth"

Eruption of the first two upper and two lower incisor teeth through the gums of a male child signals a change in his status. This is followed by the solicitation and donation of livestock on his behalf. A similar event in girls is not assigned any special significance or recognition. With the eruption of four incisor teeth, a boy is considered of sufficient age to begin learning about the habits of animals upon which he will depend for his subsistence and existence in Barabaig society. To start off his education, he should have his own herd of young animals, which he can tend and raise as he himself grows to maturity. Growing up with one's own herd is not only a lesson in animal husbandry, but also promotes an emotional identification with cattle and instills a sense of pride in the ownership of cattle—the most valued property in Barabaig society.

The amount of livestock a boy receives on the occasion of *ghat ghat*, the eruption of incisor teeth, depends upon several factors, not the least of which is the energy and power of persuasion of his mother in personally soliciting stock from her relatives as well as those of her husband. Homesteads of relatives are dispersed at considerable distance from each other and, especially during the dry season when a transhumant pattern of residence is in effect, the mother's task of solicitation becomes more difficult. The solicited livestock, known as *dug ghat*

ghat, "cattle of the sound of chewing," are brought back to the child's home where a simple ritual is performed. This ritual symbolizes the child's acceptance and claim of ownership over the donated stock. As each animal passes through the gate, the boy, held by the mother, touches each animal on its back with his "herding-stick," a stick made from the sacred fig tree. Having thus claimed ownership over the livestock, the animals are thereafter referred to as *dug geshaded,* "cattle of the tooth," and form the nucleus of his future herd. When the boy grows up, marries, and establishes a separate homestead away from his father's kraal, these cattle will be identified as *dug muhaled,* "cattle of the corral"; the names have changed to signify changes in the social status of their owner, but they are the same animals.

Contribution of *ghat ghat* cattle to a relative's son is prescribed by custom and is therefore not backed by any legal rules making it mandatory or obligatory to donate stock. Donation of stock is seen as a moral duty of kinsmen and ensures reciprocal donations of stock to one's own sons. A child receives stock from his father, from his father's full and half-brothers, and from husbands of the father's full sisters. If he has married brothers of the same or different mother and they are living in residence away from their father, the brothers will be morally obligated to give stock to their younger brother, just as they themselves received stock on occasion of their *ghat ghat.* On the mother's side, a son will receive stock from his mother, her married full and half-brothers, and her mother's brother. The acceptance of livestock from these relatives forms the basis of a system of marriage prohibitions in which the boy will be prevented from marrying any woman who is a member of a clan in which the donor is a member. Thus, the presence of their cattle in his herd reminds him of his obligation to avoid marrying or having sexual relations with a girl from the donor's clan. The transfer of cattle establishes a property relationship and in this way a kinship relationship based on blood ties is transformed into a jural relationship. Because cattle have been given, the donor acquires legal rights in matters of marriage choice by a recipient, and the recipient is legally obligated to avoid marrying his donor's clanwomen.

Co-wives of the child's mother may also be asked to contribute stock, but their donation is based on the principle of reciprocity rather than kinship. Co-wives give stock to a co-wife's son in order that their own sons may, in turn, receive stock from other mothers in the polygynous family. Donations from co-wives do not reduce their dowry cattle in number, since the livestock they contribute as *ghat ghat* are marriage cattle which the husband allocated to them but to which he still retains rights of ownership. Their own dowry cattle will never be used for increasing the economic resources of children other than their own.

Gifts of livestock (bullocks, heifers, donkeys, sheep, goats) on the occasion of *ghat ghat* may total more than ten animals, depending upon the wealth, generosity, and social and physical distance of the donors. The institution of *ghat ghat* is a cultural means by which a young Barabaig boy acquires a herd from which he eventually gains subsistence. When he marries, he transmits property to others.

The Play of Children

Continuity exists between what a Barabaig child learns through play and the basic techniques to be mastered in order to function as a capable adult. The play of Barabaig children is practice and preparation in assuming the tasks and roles of adult life. Relatively few new techniques that have not already been observed and mastered by the time a child reaches ten years of age will have to be acquired as an adult. However, vagaries of the physical and supernatural worlds will always require adjustments in coping techniques, no matter how much control a Baraband enjoys over events affecting his life.

Games of children are essentially imitative play and mimicry of adult activities. Boys learn to throw spears by first learning how to throw sticks. Accuracy in throwing is more important than distance. Boys fashion hoops out of twigs, and attempt to throw sticks through the rolling targets. When a young boy is not competing with his peers in stick games, he engages in solitary play. Constructing a kraal and huts out of sand and cow-dung, complete with livestock represented by berries or stones, he moves his "herd" in and out of the homestead. Even while walking alone, a boy imagines that he is herding cattle. He whistles, shouts, and strikes at imaginary, errant cattle, keeping them together as he walks along.

Although young girls will share herding duties in the household, they do not practice building kraals or directing cattle migrations. Girls remain closer to home and help their mothers with various domestic chores. At first, they find flat stones and grind sand as if it is maize or millet. Later, when a mother is grinding maize, a young girl will be next to her with a real grinding stone, helping her mother turn real kernels into maize meal. By the time a girl reaches four or five years of age, she is engaged in productive domestic labor. She accompanies her mother to the lake and carries back about one gallon of water in a small gourd container strapped to her back. Some girls are younger than four years of age when they learn to carry water. Small water gourds are placed on their backs and they stagger and struggle all the way back to the homestead. They apparently feel a sense of accomplishment when the water in their tiny gourds is used to prepare the evening meal.

Growing up in a Barabaig homestead means assuming greater individual responsibility at various stages in the maturation cycle of the child. Boys and girls of three years of age are given the task of herding small stock such as calves, sheep, and goats, in the vicinity of the kraal. They usually learn how to herd animals by watching older brothers or sisters, although an only child will accompany its father or mother when they are herding the stock. As they get older, children are allowed to herd larger animals. Some of these may be their own "cattle of the tooth," which have since grown to maturity.

Between the ages of four and six, boys and girls engage in sex play, imitating their parents, who do not take any precautions to prevent the children from witnessing their sex act. Since children sleep with the mother and observe the father visiting her, sex education starts early in a Barabaig household. Boys

Young boy helping his older sister tend the family herd near a crater lake.

and girls of six years of age build a small hut of sticks and grass a short distance from the kraal and engage in juvenile sex play. If they are discovered by either parent, the children will not be admonished or made to feel ashamed, although the girl will be called away to run an errand. It is a short transitional step from the sex play of children to the sexual liaisons of adolescent boys and girls. These are arranged during dances held to celebrate circumcisions and funerals—the two largest attended ceremonies in the Barabaig ritual repertory.

Preparing for Adulthood

From early childhood onward, Barabaig boys and girls are trained to perform certain tasks that they will continue to do for the rest of their lives. There are relatively few surprises in store for a Barabaig child approaching adulthood. He knows exactly what he is going to be doing as an adult, as well as the number of roles he can assume as dictated by the culture. Occupational roles are few in number, and most of them have already been performed during childhood. However, the roles of "man" and "woman" are not learned in any formal sense, but are understood by direct and repetitive observation of adults. Before a child is considered to be on its way toward becoming an adult, certain physical changes must be made in order to qualify as an adult in later years. Circumcision of boys and clitoridectomy of girls are necessary requisites for adulthood. Any boy or girl who did not submit to these operations would not be able to marry another Barabaig in later years. Genital mutilations are operations whose original rationale have been forgotten, but which are explained as a customary proce-dure in preparation for marriage.

Girls undergo clitoridectomy between the ages of two to six. No special ceremony is arranged, and the operation is performed in a homestead without any publicity. When there are a number of young girls in the neighborhood who have not been "blunted," as the Barabaig say, a female specialist is summoned by the mother of one of these children and her kraal becomes the place where the operation is performed. A small knife is used to excise the clitoris. The operation is conducted in an air of secrecy and, in many instances, the fathers of these girls were unaware that the operation had taken place until notified much later by their wives.

In contrast to clitoridectomy of girls, circumcision of boys entails an elaborate ceremony requiring the services and cooperation of large number of relatives and friends. The ceremony, *lughmadyeg balodyik*, is a three-day affair with the boys being circumcised on the last day. Large pots of honey-beer must be brewed and consumed by the elders during most of the proceedings in order for the celebration to be impressive and thus remembered. Honor is bestowed upon the owner of the homestead in which the ceremonial beer-drink takes place. His son will be the first child to submit to the knife. He and his companions will be given strips of skin taken from a newly sacrificed sheep to wear as pro-tective charms during and after their operations. Bolstered by supernatural support, they face the unknown or dimly perceived event.

When the father of an uncircumcised boy decides that he can supply a sufficient number of gallons of raw honey with which to brew honey-beer, he sends word to his married brothers and to his mother's brothers to join him in commemorating his son's impending circumcision. If the grandfathers are still alive, they will be invited to participate in the beer-drink. Arrangements are made to summon a specialist in circumcision (customarily a member of the Bisiyed clan), and homestead owners in the neighborhood and surrounding areas are no-tified of the coming event. Any father who has an uncircumcised son may bring him to the appointed kraal on the second day of the proceedings. Some boys in distant neighborhoods may hear of the planned event and run away from home to join the group of boys to be circumcized. They have withstood the jibes and taunts of young girls and circumcised boys long enough. No more will they have to be ridiculed about their penis.

For the first two days of a circumcision ceremony, preparations are made to brew large quantities of honey-beer, which will be consumed by male elders as part of the ritual. Ritual drinking of alcoholic beverages is a necessary and, to the Barabaig, vital part of every major ritual. Women are excluded from the beer-drink, as are the young men, who are ordered about by their elders and sent to cut and carry firewood, fetch water, bring gourds, and run errands. This annoys them because it takes them away from the young girls attending the dances. However, the young men obey their elders and hurriedly finish their assigned tasks in order to get back to the dance.

At dawn of the third day, some young men are sent to build a thorn-bush shelter around a solitary tree to the east of the kraal. On this particular morning, the boys will be brought to the shelter and, one by one, they will be led inside where the operation will be performed. In the meantime, they sit huddled together in a grassy spot nearby, watched by a "herdsman" whose task it is to prevent any of the boys who might change their minds from running away. They do not receive any formal instruction or education during the three-day period. After circumcision, they will not stay together or identify with each other as a permanent group. Ages of the boys range from two to ten years. This is a reflection of the transhumant pattern of residence and the limited opportunity for circumcision, especially where timing is concerned. Of course, a father or an uncircumcised son may postpone decision to participate in a local circumcision, but this is a matter of individual choice. More often, a father will grasp the opportunity to have his son circumcised, but only if he does not contemplate holding a circumcision ceremony in his own homestead. Many fathers do not have the necessary wealth to furnish raw honey for the beer-brewing. A memorable beer-drink is one in which thirty or more gallons of raw honey produces over 200 gallons of honey-beer. Honey-beer is considered sacred, and the state of intoxication it produces is apparently similar to religious ecstasy, although the Barabaig do not phrase their feelings in exactly these terms.

Unlike other East African societies in which boys are required to remain stoic and impassive during the operation, Barabaig boys are allowed to react to pain and many scream pitifully, "Take my father, take my mother, but leave me alone." or "I'll never do it again." Older boys hurl obscenities at the circumciser. After the operation, each boy is given a drink of raw cow's blood and milk to help him recuperate. When the last boy has been circumcised, elders form a group and dance and sing around the shelter and then head toward the kraal to refill their drinking gourds. The boys sit disconsolately in the shelter awaiting nightfall when they will be brought into the kraal. In the morning, after being examined by the circumciser for possible signs of infection, the boys are released to return to their homesteads.

Newly circumcised boys enjoy a one-month period of convalescence and freedom during which they are relieved of all herding duties and other chores. They wander around the neighborhood terrorizing young girls. Brandishing a large thorn switch, they exact tribute, mostly brass bangles or strings of beads, from young girls who are fearful of being beaten. Older girls laugh and run away, which is not the kind of reaction the boys expect. After one month of ritual tyranny, the boys tire of it, take up their herding sticks and resume their path toward adulthood.

Learning to Compete

Growing up in Barabaig society means becoming aware of the numerous problems that exist and the cultural solutions to these problems. A child soon learns the lesson that constant vigilance and opportunism is the price of survival. The physical and social environments are things to be reckoned with and brought under control. However, in order to achieve control it is necessary to compete against other individuals and families for scarce resources. For the Barabaig, grass for their cattle is a valuable resource; it is valuable because it is scarce, especially during the dry season. If a Barabaig cattle-herder is adequately exploiting the physical environment, he is usually doing it at the expense of others. Thus, a kind of zero-sum game exists in which the gains of one cattle-herder are the losses of another. Each family and its herd is a separate, self-sufficient, economic unit competing against like units. In a semi-arid environment in which man's biological survival is closely tied to his ability to locate adequate grazing for his cattle to feed on, it is not surprising that a spirit of competition rather than cooperation should be fostered and encouraged. At no time is this more apparent than during the dry season, when grazing areas turn into dust bowls and gale-force winds turn the amiability and sociability of the Barabaig into anger and frustration. Whatever cooperation exists at this time is found among close relatives and friends. Physical environment and the techniques by which it is exploited are two of a number of determinants contributing to Barabaig personality formation.

To live in Barabaig society is to be exposed to countless situations in which a person's estimation of his ability and self-worth is challenged and publicly exposed. While physical environment and the behavioral requirements of a technology built around the maintenance and control of domesticated cattle are determinants of personality characteristics of the Barabaig, they alone cannot account for a Baraband's readiness to respond in an aggressive manner, verbally and physically. Just as he is ever-watchful and defensive with regard to the welfare of his cattle herd, so he is defensive concerning his social position and personal self-esteem. Social prestige, like cattle, is scarce among the Barabaig. Most prestige must be acquired through personal accomplishments rather than accident of birth. Thus a great deal of pressure is put on the individual to compete against others for social recognition from fellow tribesmen.

"Enemy of the People"

Lifelong prestige is awarded to any man who has killed an "enemy of the people." The lion, elephant, rhino, cape buffalo, and alien tribesmen are all considered "enemies," and the killer of one of these status animals is rewarded with gifts of livestock from his relatives and people living in the vicinity of the kill. In addition to economic gain in the form of cattle, a killer or *ghadyirochand* is entitled to wear special regalia that visibly identify him as a "killer." He dons a

Killer of an "Enemy of the People." He wears a heavily-beaded cap with brass "lion's tail."

heavily beaded leather cap with a long curving strip of brass symbolizing the tail of a lion. Brass neck coils, ear coils, and finger-rings customarily worn by women are worn for a few weeks while the man makes the rounds of his relatives' homesteads and neighborhood to solicit livestock for having made a kill.

Upon making a kill, the young man returns to his parents' kraal and sits down outside the gate, singing his kill-song, *ranginod*, while waiting for his father and mother to give him cows. Having received offers of cows, he walks through the kraal gate and his head is anointed with butter. The next day he goes out to collect his lover and her girl friends who will accompany him on his journey to solicit gifts. He adorns himself with women's ornaments, which symbolize that he is like a woman who has given birth. Killing an enemy of the people and giving birth are symbolically equated. The killer of an enemy must observe a convalescence period for having given "birth," and is restricted from touching food or doing any work. However, he is allowed to join dance groups and is not prohibited from other social contacts. As he goes from place to place, he sings his kill-song and waves his shield in front of his mouth, giving his voice a quavering sound. People honor him by throwing butter that spatters his shield, his face and clothes. After about one month, he removes most of the female ornamentation, with the exception of the brass finger-rings. These will be worn for a lifetime as visual evidence of his status.

Ritual Murder

Neighboring tribesmen are also considered enemies of the people, and killing one of their members is a highly commendable deed. This deed warrants the reward of gifts of livestock and social prestige bestowed upon the killer by members of his own society. The concept of murder is relative to one's own society.

"Ritual murder" of neighboring tribesmen has a long history among the Barabaig and goes back to the period of German colonial rule. It may be a continuation, on an individual basis, of the rivalry generated between clans before German military intervention put a stop to the Masai wars. During the British administration, scores of young Barabaig killers have been caught, brought to trial, sentenced, and hanged with very little deterring effect on the incidence of ritual killings or its supporting cultural patterns and social institutions.

Motives for killing an alien tribesman are many and varied, depending upon individual circumstances or social situations. While a profit motive may be behind some of the killings, many occur after some social event has spurred or goaded an individual into seeking out a victim. Traditionally, the WaNyaturu, WaNyiramba, and WaIsanzu, all Bantu-speaking tribes, have been the principal targets of ritual killing. Long-standing feuds and border disputes over land and water rights have perpetuated some of the hostility of the Barabaig toward their Bantu neighbors. Confiscations of Barabaig cattle by government authorities backing WaNyaturu claims of border violations and intrusions have incensed some Barabaig youth to retaliate by murdering indiscriminately. Moreover, the Barabaig personality trait of being "quick to anger and slow to forget" is conducive to the triggering of smoldering resentment and mounting frustration.

Instigation to commit "ritual murder" occurs under a number of different social conditions, all of which contribute to a "quick" decision to kill. Rivalries between young girls and their lovers, between wives of different clansmen, and between rival clansmen, set the stage for an expedition to murder.

Rivalries exist between young girls who "buy" the kills of their lovers with sexual favors. A girl often provokes a young man into setting out to make a kill. She may taunt and ridicule a potential lover by telling him that he has not killed anything for her. A girl may enrage her lover by taking away his spear and striking its iron blade against a rock or attempting to spear a boulder. This is her way of showing him that his spear is next to useless. He may become so enraged that he will go to some of his friends to organize a hunt for a status animal. If there is difficulty in locating a lion, elephant, rhino, or cape buffalo, there is always an opportunity to find an unsuspecting alien tribesman in the border area.

Rivalry and ridicule are the components of many songs and dances of Barabaig men and women. In women's dance groups, women sing about the daring exploits of former lovers or young men of their husbands' clans by recounting the number of kills credited to the men in their songs. Some women jibe and ridicule other women who are temporarily shamed into silence. Upon returning home, these "vanquished" women will taunt and ridicule their husband's younger brothers or their own sons.

Public ridicule perpetuates the institution of killing "status animals" or "enemies of the people" by permeating many of the social occasions when large groups of people gather to perform some commemorative or status ritual (such as a funeral or circumcision, which attracts hundreds of persons many of whom walk long distances to attend). During a young people's dance (a mixed dance of girls and young men) the dance arena may suddenly be cleared by the shouts of a young man calling for a stick dance, *jibod dabit*. In a stick dance, young men compete against each other for honor and prestige. Men form a circle and one young man steps forward singing a song of praise for his kill. He throws down one stick to signify his kill and a second stick to symbolize his spear. This is a challenge for others to step forward and best his claim. Another man may attempt to rival him by throwing down two sticks plus the "spear stick." If the first killer does not have any additional sticks to throw down, he is defeated and moves back into the crowd. Sometimes, a third dancer comes forward to outrival the kills of the other two. Shaming of a rival during a *jibod dabit* may force a young man to go immediately to a neighboring tribal area to seek out an "enemy of the people."

A young man setting out to kill an alien tribesman usually gathers a small group of friends who accompany him as helpers and witnesses. After spearing a neighboring tribesman, usually a WaNyaturu, he cuts off the nose and ear from the corpse to bring back as proof of his kill, the word of his witnesses not being sufficient evidence to substantiate his claim. These trophies are then shown to his girl friend to further verify his deed. He is now ready to receive *dug gimard*, "cattle of the butter anointment," from his parents and relatives and those homesteads nearest the kill.

British administrators believed that Barabaig ritual murders followed a fixed pattern and invariably the killers were younger sons of lesser wives who were in an economically disadvantageous position in the family hierarchy. Basic motive of economic gain in cattle was singled out as the chief reason for ritual murder. While the pursuit of economic gain by younger brothers of mothers with lesser rank in a polygynous family is a possible motive for some killers, it is not always so. In 1957, two young men, Subaida and Ghamung, were hanged in the government prison at Dodoma, Tanganyika, for the murder of a MuNyaturu at Muunga in the Singida District. Although Ghamung was a younger son of a lesser wife, Subaida was not only the first son of the first wife and thus heir to both his father's and mother's cattle-holdings, but also the future ritual leader of his clan, the Basaŋinyek. Considering all of the advantages—social, economic, and political—enjoyed by Subaida, it would be misleading to assign economic motive as the reason for his participation in ritual murder.

Ritual murder of alien tribesmen continues to the present day, but the newly independent government of Tanzania is prepared to take steps to stop it. It is one traditional custom of the African heritage that will not be tolerated or preserved.

6

Marriage and Property Relations

Arranging a Marriage

THERE ARE SEVERAL STAGES through which every Barabaig marriage proceeds, from the time of its inception until its termination either in divorce or death. A series of livestock transactions is an integral part of the marriage system and forms the legal basis upon which the marriage rests.

When a girl has reached what is considered a marriageable age, usually marked by breast development, there may be several prospective suitors ready to make known their intentions of marriage. There is a considerable difference in the marrying age of girls and boys. Marriageable age for girls is around 13 or 14 years of age. Rarely does a girl marry before the onset of puberty and rarely is she still unmarried after reaching 20 years of age. Boys marry much later in life, usually around 24 years of age. Earlier marriages do occur, although they were relatively infrequent in the past and appear today as a modern innovation. Formerly, young men served as warriors, and married life was reserved for older men. It was believed that married life would be a distraction that would seriously affect the discipline and fighting ability of the warriors.

In the past, all marriages were arranged by the parents of the boy and girl, but today if a young man is attracted by a girl he wishes to marry, he notifies his father, his mother, or his mother's brother, who then investigates the kinship and economic background of the girl's family. Should the father disapprove of his son's choice of potential marriage mate, the son will usually abide by his father's decision, at least as long as he is living in his father's homestead and is under his authority. It is also economically wise to conform to his father's ruling since he is partly dependent on him for the donation of livestock that will legally establish the marriage.

The order of marriage for sons in a polygynous family follows the rule of seniority. Each family segment or hut-group consisting of a mother and her children is a separate economic unit in terms of its property holdings, and each segment regulates the order of marriage of sons and daughters. In every hut-group the oldest son marries before his younger full brother, but not necessarily before a half-brother from a different hut-group. While the order of marriage of sons is determined by order of birth to a particular mother, the marriage order for the daughters is not rigidly regulated. Although it is desirable that the oldest daughter in a hut-group should marry before any of her full sisters, the opportunity to marry takes precedence over seniority. There is no fixed order of marriage for daughters of different mothers.

Every Barabaig girl must marry, whether or not she is physically desirable. Crippled, deformed, and demented girls must have a wedding in order for them to be eligible to wear the *hananŋwend,* a pleated leather skirt having magico-religious significance since it was designed by Udameselgwa, the female deity and patroness of Barabaig women. Also, the wearing of a skirt is mandatory in order to prevent exposure of genitalia of mature women. There are no unmarried women in Barabaig society.

Preliminary to any extensive economic negotiations with a girl's family, each prospective suitor asks his father, brothers, mother's brothers, and friends to arrange a series of meetings with the girl's father, brothers, and neighbors in order to determine whether there are any kinship connections between the two families. First, he is prohibited from marrying any girl from his own clan. To do so would be considered incestuous, *nyamod,* and he would be subject to a cattle fine levied by his clan elders. Second, he cannot marry any girl who is a member of his mother's clan, his grandmothers' clans, or his great-grandmothers' clans. This means that there may be seven clans, plus his own clan, from which he cannot select a marriage mate. The inquiry to establish a marriage suit is allowed to continue if neither the girl nor her intended suitor share a common clan tie.

The character, reputation, and wealth of the girl's immediate family are also of concern to the potential suitor. Similarly, the girl's parents are also interested in trying to determine the kind of in-law relatiohs likely to be established by her marriage to a particular young man. Harmonious in-law relations are considered more important than the relative wealth of each family. Possession of wealth by either family usually does not cancel out the social disadvantages of a marriage alliance with dim prospects of harmonious relations. Girls from families with reputations for constant quarreling and bickering are usually not selected as first marriage choice by potential suitors.

Choice of marriage partner is also complicated by the fact that young men from large clans with mothers and grandmothers from large clans are restricted to choosing girls from small clans with severe limitations because of the number of girls available. Of course, the opposite is also true. Men from clans with small memberships have a wider choice when they marry into one of the larger clans. But, once a man marries a woman from a large clan, his sons will again be restricted because they are not allowed to marry girls from their mother's clan. Therefore, demographic restrictions concerning the number of potential marriage mates available under a culturally proscribed system of marriage may force its young people to either choose other appropriate alternatives or create new ones.

Some Barabaig men have married outside their tribe, but there are advantages and disadvantages to marriages of this kind. While the husband of a foreign wife does not have to give bridewealth (a payment of cattle to the girl's parents) she, in turn, does not bring with her any dowry cattle. She is considered an alien, but her children will be Barabaig. Children of a non-Barabaig mother usually receive no economic support in the form of cattle gifts from their mother's brother, a traditional Barabaig source of livestock donations. Therefore, there are strong economic arguments for marrying within Barabaig society, although a number of young men married Iraqw girls in order to avoid payment of bridewealth only to find later that they started a process of intermarriage and infiltration of Iraqw people into Barabaig territory, thus necessitating a different ecological adjustment to their physical environment.

Perhaps a more drastic solution to the problem of limited marriage choice has been to defy the traditional system of marriage. Even though a marriage suit has been arranged by a girl's parents, it does not necessarily mean that the marriage will take place. Strong-willed girls have defied their parents and have eloped with young men of their choice. A girl may run away from home and go to live in her lover's homestead or they both may go to his mother's brother's homestead. Her brother, who is usually her confidant, knows the name of the man with whom she eloped and may go to his kraal to return his sister. However, if she refuses to reconsider her choice of marriage mate and if her parents approve of the young man, the normal steps to marriage will be followed, but only after a fine of six barrels of honey has been imposed on the young man because he caused the girl's father to "step on thorns" in his search for his missing daughter.

Some elopements do not result in an acceptable marriage alliance. Elopement with a girl to whom marriage is considered incestuous is rare, but has occurred. In 1958, a young man fell in love with a girl who, according to kinship and generational reckoning, could be his "daughter." Both his and her parents objected to their plans for marriage on the grounds that it would be a "sin" punishable by some supernatural accident. The couple ignored their parents' protests and eloped to his mother's brother's homestead where they convinced the uncle of their determination to marry despite any threat. After a brief "wedding" ritual, the couple left the kraal and went into hiding when they learned that a tribal council of elders, *girgwaged getabarak* or "council of the wide tree," was meeting to discuss possible steps to take against them. Elders complained that this incident could set a bad precedent by giving other young men ideas about marrying girls who are not marriageable because it would be considered incestuous or sinful. Groups of men gathered under shade trees and discussed the elopement. Many shook their heads and predicted that the couple would die a horrible death, struck down by an angry God.

Accepting a Suitor

Several suitors are usually available, but selection of the future husband is difficult because each suitor may have different qualifications. Some may come from large wealthy clans who are politically influential. Personal character of the boy and his family are also considerations, especially in establishing amicable in-law relations. The girl's father, mother, brothers, and mother's brothers are consulted in a family council, and by a process of elimination two suitors are chosen. The man finally accepted as the future husband of the girl is invited to her homestead where a ritual takes place, setting the pattern of hospitality for future social relations between in-laws. He is brought into his future mother-in-law's room and is purposely directed to sit on her bed and partake of food specially prepared for him by the girl's mother. This ritual is designed to serve as a rapprochement between the future son-in-law and mother-in-law. Barabaig society is characteristically free of any institutionalized mother-in-law avoidance patterns. Whenever a son-in-law enters the kraal of his mother-in-law, she will stop her work and immediately prepare a meal for him. If they encounter each other while walking to some destination, the son-in-law will approach her and engage in conversation. Generally speaking, there appears to be a deliberate attempt by Barabaig to maintain contact and communication between in-laws, with the exception of relations between the girl and her husband's father where there is a pattern of avoidance or social distance. Even the husband is not permitted to talk with his future bride. He limits his conversation to her family and avoids meeting her until the day he arrives to "capture the bride."

Capture of the Bride

Before dawn on the morning when the prospective groom is to claim his bride, he and a group of friends go to the girl's homestead. Arrangements have been made in advance, usually with the girl's mother or brother, to open the kraal gate by removing the thorn-bush that projects outward and serves as a barrier. The strategy of capturing the bride is called *lugod*, the same term used to denote a war maneuver or raid. Object of the maneuvering is to place a string of red and blue beads, having magico-religious significance, around the girl's neck. Once the *ghadyich'k*, the beads, are around the girl's neck, it signals the end of her residence in her father's kraal and the beginning of betrothal residence with the future groom and his parents.

Capture of the bride does not usually proceed smoothly, and a struggle may ensue when the girl tries to prevent the beads from being slipped over her head and around her neck. In her resistance and reluctance to surrender, she may take a stick and try to beat away the bridegroom and his helpers. Other girls in the family join in to help her and the show of resistance may assume the appearance of battle. On some occasions, the struggle becomes so violent that the string of beads is broken and the "capture" delayed until the beads are collected and restrung. Once the beads are around the girl's neck, the girl is supposed to be pacified and resigned to her fate.

For a Barabaig girl, her "capture" marks the end of her membership in the peer group of young girls and the severance of relations with her lover. Barabaig girls generally do not marry lovers. She can no longer participate in the subculture of the generation group of young men and unmarried girls who arrange secret meetings, trysts, and conduct councils where violators of the young people's ethical code are brought to trial for breach of good conduct. After her capture, the girl no longer associates with the young girls' group and severs all ties with the group of young people. Her place is with the women and their groups.

News of a girl's "capture" reaches the young girls of the neighborhood, who assemble at her homestead to "mourn her death." The girls are called *shogodik*, the same term used to designate a group of mourners on the occasion of death in the neighborhood. Inside the girl's room, the girls deprecate her future husband and tell her about all the misfortune she is going to have. They start to lament, each girl trying to out-rival the laments of other girls. Each girl tells about the deeds of her lover and identifies with him when she cries, "I killed a lion." "I killed an enemy." The crying continues for an hour or more, during which time some of the girls' voices become hoarse and strained. When the time approaches for the girl to leave her home for the homestead of her future husband, she tells the girls, "All this finished. I cannot help you anymore. Good-bye, my ostriches." From this day on, she no longer associates with her former girlhood companions.

Bridewealth

The transfer and exchange of cattle between individuals and groups is never more complex or elaborate in Barabaig society than on the occasion of marriage. Starting with the betrothal and moving through time and space to the final stages of marriage, a series of livestock transactions take place. These establish certain social relationships and define their moral and legal bases. Just as Barabaig marriage and the family moves through stages of development, so the rights of ownership and residence of cattle change concomitantly. Names that designate certain groups of cattle change in accordance with their passage from individual to individual, or as the Barabaig conceive it, from one group to another, since the individual is in reality a legal and social representative of his lineage and clan and his cattle are likewise deemed representative of lineage and clan cattle.

A distinction must be drawn between bridewealth cattle and marriage cattle. Bridewealth for the Barabaig is the transfer of cattle from the family of the bridegroom to the family of the bride. Bridewealth cattle do not contribute to the economic support of the family formed by the marriage but are used to establish certain rights. By payment of bridewealth, a husband gains the right to determine marriage residence. It is the girl who must leave her family and go to live with her husband's parents. He also gains rights over the sexual and procreative capacity of his wife. Children born of the marriage belong to him and, in case of divorce, the wife returns back to her parents without her children. The husband also gains certain rights over the domestic labor of his wife but this may be temporarily suspended when her family imposes a coercive sanction against her husband because he has been mistreating her or has been insubordinate to or caused physical injury to her relatives or members of her natal clan.

Numerous economic and noneconomic explanations have been advanced by anthropologists concerning the institution of bridewealth. One explanation which has received wide acceptance is to the effect that bridewealth is a compensation paid to a girl's family for the economic loss they sustain because a valuable producer in the economic life of her group has been taken away. Among the Barabaig, bridewealth is so nominal, consisting of one heifer, called *ded gadyeld*, that it cannot be considered as a compensation for economic loss of a daughter's services. As a matter of fact, there is an economic loss but it is measured in terms of the dowry cattle which the daughter will take away from her family and lineage. Barabaig fathers complain that it is unprofitable to have daughters because they take away livestock from the clan, lineage, and family, and distribute them to their offspring who will be members of a different clan, her husband's clan. Fathers seem to forget that they profited in a similar way from their wives' dowry cattle. Another reason why the birth of daughters is considered to be an unfortunate event is due to the fact that only male offspring can continue the membership and existence of a clan or lineage. Daughters will be mothers of children who will belong to other clans. Paradoxically, the fertility of a man's wives in producing daughters may lead to the extinction of his lineage and the dispersion of his lineage stock.

Payment of bridewealth is the responsibility of the groom's father as long as the son is living in the father's kraal. As soon as a married son moves away to establish an independent homestead, it will be the son's responsibility to furnish the bridewealth for his second wife, and subsequent wives. Paternal obligation to supply bridewealth exists only for sons living in their father's homestead.

While Barabaig society may be generally considered wealthy, in terms of the size of tribal and individual livestock holdings, the nominal payment of one heifer does not increase the incidence of polygyny. A cow must have certain requisite qualifications before it can be used in a bridewealth transaction. Since most Barabaig cows fail to meet these requisites, an animal which can qualify is a scarce resource. First, the cow must be all of one color—all black, all white, all brown, and so forth. If any other color spot appears on any part of the animal's head, body, or legs, the animal is judged ineligible for selection as bridewealth. Secondly, the cow must be a heifer, that is, one which has never calved. This means that the heifer would be between two to three years of age. A third requisite, fertility, must be met when the animal is quartered in the in-law's kraal. A barren cow will be returned and a fertile animal sent as a replacement. If the future bridegroom or his family does not own an animal with the proper specifications, several courses of action are possible. They may exchange one of their multicolored cows for a single colored heifer belonging to one of their clan members or relatives. Or, the bridewealth payment may be deferred, with the consent of the in-laws, until such time as the family herd of the bridegroom produces a suitable animal. While there is some advantage to deferred payment, this option is not usually exercised because it can create more problems than it solves. If the payment of bridewealth is not made before a wife gives birth, her father or brother can legally claim the child born of the marriage. A great deal of excitement is generated when a husband experiences difficulty in locating a suitable animal to give as bridewealth and his wife is in her last month of pregnancy. It is at times like these that an individual turns to his kinsmen to solicit their aid. Invariably, an animal is found bearing the necessary qualifications in the herd of some kinsman who has been saving it for his son, or for his own use to obtain another wife. Scarcity of cows with requisite qualifications for bridewealth limits the incidence of polygyny.

Unlike other East African cattle-herding societies which require larger payments of bridewealth, the Barabaig's nominal payment of one heifer does not create any problem of distribution. The bridewealth cow, *ded gadyeld*, is the possession of the girl's eldest full brother. If she has not a full brother, the cow will be kept by her father who has temporary holding rights over the animal.

The presence of the husband's cow in the herd of his in-laws and some of the wife's family cattle in the husband's herd serve as constant reminders of the marriage bond established between the two families. Full rights of ownership over the *ded gadyeld*, are not conveyed until the girl gives birth to a son, which then prevents the return of any cattle used in marriage transactions. The birth of a son stabilizes the marriage and transfers full ownership of the bridewealth cow as well as dowry cattle to the respective in-law households. In cases of divorce or death of a wife, her dowry cattle belong to her son. If there is no son, then both the bridewealth cow and dowry cattle are returnable to their original owners.

Unlike the Lovedu society of the Transvaal, a Baraband cannot use his sister's bridewealth to obtain a wife of his own. He cannot remove his sister's *ded gadyeld* from his herd but he can sell, exchange, or sacrifice any of the progeny of the bridewealth cow. Continued fertility of the bridewealth cow increases the size of the wife's brother's herd.

In contrast to the bridewealth payment to the brother, a girl's father and mother receive only the *maled anog*, "honey of the breast milk," a small barrel of honey which is an essential part of the marriage transaction but does not constitute a part of the bridewealth since it is never returnable to the husband.

In societies with high bridewealth payments, the bride's family is generally anxious for the marriage to endure because they are reluctant to return bridewealth which may already have been used for other purposes. In contrast, among the Barabaig, it is the groom's family who is concerned that the marriage succeeds, since the girl's dowry cattle will become the possession of her son, or sons, and therefore become new additions to clan and lineage livestock holdings.

Marriage Cattle

Every Barabaig marriage must be founded on an economic base involving the control of livestock resources. Marriage cattle are those animals which furnish subsistence for the husband and wife and which are allocated to them by their kin. Included in the family herd will be cattle donated by the wife's relatives as dowry and cattle received by the husband from his family. Each group of animals are differentiated by a reference name and these names change through time as the marriage proceeds from its inception, consolidation, and termination.

The journey of a girl from her parents' homestead to the homestead of her future husband and his parents is marked by a series of livestock transactions. Her passage is halted at various stages of the journey by gift offers of cattle which are promised her by various donors. Before she exits through the gate of her home and before she enters her new home with her in-laws, a girl receives offers of livestock from both family groups.

On the day of the "capture of the bride," the girl and her family enter into negotiations concerning the dowry cattle she is entitled to receive as part of the cattle which will comprise her family herd. A leather thong, used as a cow tether, is attached to her cape and as she is slowly led through the kraal gate she refuses to pass through until an offer of cattle is made by her father, mother, and married full brothers. Each individual contributes according to his ability to sustain loss of stock, personal regard for the girl, and closeness of kinship ties. As she stands in the gateway, listening to the names of the livestock being offered to her as dowry, she accepts or refuses the offers according to her knowledge of the animals. She knows which cows are good milch cows, which bulls are progeny from good milch cows, for she has spent much time tending the family herd and she knows the good and bad qualities of every animal. After she finally accepts a number of offers of cattle, she leaves her old sandals near the gate and steps into a new pair given to her by her future husband. Fitted with a new pair of sandals for her new journey into married life, she pauses outside the kraal while a group of girls and women take off some of their bead necklaces and place them around her neck. She is given a gourd bowl, containing a mixture of red ochre and butter, from which she will periodically anoint her body during her betrothal period spent in residence at her future husband's homestead. The red ochre anointment has a special magico-religious significance, the rationale of which has been forgotten. It is one of the practices which is best explained with the words, "It is custom."

When Udahonda was married, she was offered 16 head of cattle but some of these offers proved difficult to collect when her husband arrived at the homesteads of her relatives to solicit the stock which were promised her. Offers of livestock sometimes prove to be a deception designed to facilitate the departure of the girl who is generally reluctant to leave her family. Generally, daughters of wealthy cattle owners receive the dowry cattle they have been promised because it is a matter of pride and social prestige. Later on, the cattle owner can boast about the number of dowry cattle he has given to his daughters, and his reputation and social stature will increase proportionately.

The range of dowry among the Barabaig may be between 2 to 40 head of livestock, depending on a number of factors. Communication between kin is hampered by physical distance, climate, and frequency of moving of homesteads, especially during the dry season. Families with large herds must move more often than families with small herds. It is the family with a large herd that is in the best economic position to donate dowry cattle to a sister or first cousin, the latter contributing because they at one time probably received stock from the girl's parents. Locating the whereabouts of relatives during the dry season may entail a lengthy investigation. If they cannot be brought to the girl's homestead at the time when she is ready to depart for her in-law's kraal they are not obligated to contribute dowry.

Upon arrival at her future husband's kraal, she pauses outside the gate and waits for her father-in-law to offer her *detosht*, "cow of the gate," which she accepts before entering the gate. She is also given a pleated leather skirt, *hananŋwend,* a symbol of marital status. Although the wedding ceremony may be weeks away, the marriage transactions have reached a point where her marital status is a foregone conclusion. Not even the discovery of a genealogical tie between her kin and her future husband's kin can change the course of marriage. If such a situation would occur, the wedding would be allowed to take place and a divorce would follow the next day.

During her betrothal period in residence with her mother-in-law, the girl is instructed in family customs and generally treated as incompetent. Her mother-in-law cooks for her and she is not allowed to milk any of the family's cows. She avoids looking at or speaking to her father-in-law, and only catches glimpses of her future husband. Only after she has been given a new name, a "milk name" chosen by her husband, or his father or mother, and is offered milch cows and a drink of milk from the family herd will her ritual semi-isolation come to an end. Enough butter has been collected during her betrothal period and the day of the wedding is set.

Wedding

Weddings occur more frequently in the rainy season than during the dry season when it is more difficult to accumulate enough butter for all the ritual needs of a wedding. Butter has a magico-religious significance when used as an anointment during ritual. Large quantities of butter are needed to smear the body of the bride and her female relatives who are wedding guests.

Festivities surrounding the wedding last three days and are attended by relatives of the bride and groom and women of the neighborhood. Each day, neighborhood women gather to dance and sing their obscene boasts, which may curiously be associated with the promotion of fertility. Or, the ritual obscenity may be an overt expression of female hostility towards men. Men avoid the dance area when the *dumd dumod*, "dance of the penis," is in progress. Indeed, men are generally considered "outsiders" at weddings and do not participate in any of the rituals. The bridegroom may brew some honey-beer and invite a few male friends to a beer-drink but otherwise he does not participate in any of the wedding rituals performed by the group of women.

On the third and last day of the wedding, the bride is offered some livestock, *dug gihimd* or "cattle to show," by her husband, but these usually prove to be a deception because included in the count are cows that had previously been offered to her when she received her "milk name."

In the afternoon of the third day, one of the milch cows in the bridegroom's herd is selected by him and presented to the bride for her first milking chore in her in-law's homestead. During her betrothal residence she had been subject to a milking taboo, but this did not prevent her from learning about the milk yield of her husband's cows. When offered the *detawaght* or "Cow of the red ochre," the bride may refuse it if she knows that the cow has a poor milk yield. She continues to refuse other offerings until she receives a good milch cow. Before milking the cow, the bride takes some of the red ochre and butter that has been smeared on her head during one of the rituals and with her fingers smears the mixture on the back of the cow. By this action, she removes the milking taboo she has observed during her betrothal period.

Consummation of marriage usually takes place in the evening of the third day. The bride is instructed by the women of the household to resist the sexual advances of the husband. When her husband arrives at the special hut built in the cattle corral, a verbal exchange takes place in which the bride is offered a payment of cattle, *dug aba ga*, "cattle of the room," for allowing sexual embrace. The husband promises her cattle, but it usually proves to be a deception.

Marriage must be consummated before either the bride or groom is allowed to participate in normal domestic activities around the homestead. The groom's mother, or his first wife if he is a polygynist, pours milk into a gourd called a *ghaded ŋushand* or "gourd of the spittle," which supposedly contains the "medicine" concocted by Udameselgwa, the female deity. This is thought to be a magical potion that entices men to accept the concept of marriage. When the couple have consummated the marriage, the husband uncovers the gourd and takes a drink. He then offers the gourd to his wife, who pretends to taste it. The gourd is placed near the door of the hut, and in the morning the husband's mother, or his first wife, examines the level of the milk in the gourd; a change in the milk level is verification of consummation of marriage.

In-laws

Social relations of a wife with her husband's family are of a different character and emotional tone than those of a husband towards his wife's parents and relatives. Although both husband and wife observe certain rules of etiquette with regard to each other's family, a wife is required to follow certain rules of avoidance or respect which are not in effect for her husband in relations with her family.

While in residence with her intended husband's family, the betrothed girl observes strict rules governing her conduct in the presence of her father-in-law. She avoids speaking to him, and if spoken to she adopts a deferential attitude and feigns modesty. With her mother-in-law, the girl behaves in a more relaxed manner, but still maintains an air of self-effacement. She is not treated as an equal, but as a minor who must be taught the customs of the family culture. Indeed, her lower social status is reflected in having to observe a personal name taboo, *giŋawakshod,* throughout her bethrothal and marriage.

Upon marriage, a woman must alter her normal speech habits and become guarded in her use of many common words. She is not permitted to use any words that are either identical with, or resemble even remotely, the personal names of her husband's dead relatives. This personal name taboo presents problems of communication by forcing a wife to restrict her normal speech even when referring to common actions and objects in her social and physical environment. If one of her husband's dead relatives was named Gidamadyod (*Gid* is a masculine name prefix and *madyod* means medicine), she cannot use the common word for medicine, but must resort to some circumlocution (such as "thing that cures") whenever she asks for or refers to medicine. In order to know which words must be avoided, she learns the personal names of all her husband's dead relatives from her mother-in-law as part of her education in family ways.

The personal name taboo is observed as a mark of respect and deference to be shown to her living in-laws. It is also a restriction that prevents her from unwittingly summoning the ancestral spirits of her husband's dead relatives. There is a strong belief that any violation of the personal name taboo will cause the spirits to ascend from the underworld and, through the medium of fire, will set her leather skirt afire when she is cooking. If she inadvertently speaks one of the forbidden words, she excuses herself by biting her beads and exclaiming aloud, "I have mistakenly called you." Only during labor pains and difficult childbirth will she deliberately call out the forbidden names in order to summon assistance of the ancestral spirits. A relaxation of her personal name taboo also occurs after the woman has given birth to two sons. In case of divorce, she is no longer bound to observe the name taboo, but in the event of remarriage she will acquire another set of name prohibitions.

Social tension between a woman and her in-laws is lessened more and more as she produces more male children to perpetuate her husband's and father-in-law's lineage and clan. Until she proves her ability to bear children, especially male children, a wife is subject to a certain amount of tension and anxiety created by her husband and his relatives. Although a woman's relationship with her mother-in-law is strengthened through daily contact and interaction, she avoids her father-in-law and shows him proper respect by looking away from him whenever he speaks to her, which is seldom. A daughter-in-law who would look into the eyes of her husband's father would be considered brazen and lacking in etiquette. For observing an attitude of deference, a girl might receive additional stock from her father-in-law when it came time to offer her livestock during the "milk name" ritual. A father-in-law's personal estimation of the girl's qualities is enhanced by her proper demeanor and is reflected in the amount of his donation.

While differences in sex may account for some of the restrictions placed on the father-in-law and daughter-in-law relationship, the same explanation cannot be extended to the relationship between the mother-in-law and son-in-law, which is not characterized by any social barrier of customary avoidance or strong deference. Instead, there is a marked congeniality and commensality between a man and his wife's mother. Closing social distance rather than maintaining it are the objectives of various patterns of interaction between mother-in-law and son-in-law. She is more of a friend to her daughter's husband than a socially remote parent who must be avoided in order to protect the marriage. However, relations between a son-in-law and father-in-law are cautious and well-considered, as is customary for any relation between persons of different generations. A husband shows deference to his father-in-law and some of his wife's brothers, but he usually develops a close friendship with his wife's oldest brother. It is not unusual for a man to move his homestead into the neighborhood of his senior brother-in-law. Indeed, each man has cattle belonging to the other in his own herd. A man's bridewealth cow and her offspring will be in the herd of his wife's brother and the dowry cattle belonging to the wife's brother and given to his sister will be in his sister's husband's herd. So, they follow the progress of each other's livestock donations and share common interests in the welfare of their herds. While there is friendly joking permitted between a man and his wife's brother, he is more often the butt of a joke. Relations between in-laws should be on the friendliest of terms, supportive, and relatively free of tension but personality differences may operate to produce discord rather than harmony. In this instance, a man has but to move his family and herd to a new location and, if he has other wives, he can devaluate one brother-in-law relationship and upgrade another. Reliance on cattle gives him a physical mobility and choice in social relations which sedentary societies practicing horticulture do not afford its members.

Continuing a Marriage

Death of a spouse does not mean the end of a Barabaig marriage. There are cultural provisions made for the continuance of a marriage despite the death of a husband or wife. The levirate, as it is referred to by cultural anthropologists, is a cultural solution designed to perpetuate the marriage of a deceased husband by allowing his surviving wives and their children to live with one of the deceased husband's married brothers, usually the eldest. A wife is expected to continue to bear children in her deceased husband's name, although living in the kraal of his surviving brother. Her marriage persists as long as the property relationship established by the transfer of bridewealth remains unchanged.

Neither the widow nor her late husband's brothers are legally obligated to enter into leviratic union. The levirate is only one of a number of possible alternatives available as solutions to the problem of adult, heterosexual, domestic life. A leviratic union is established only with the consent of both principals involved in the alliance. If the brother of the deceased husband, or the widow herself, does not wish to enter into a leviratic alliance, the woman's marriage is dissolved and she is free to marry a man from a clan other than the one to which her late husband belonged.

There are a number of compelling reasons why either the widow or her deceased husband's brother would choose to accept leviratic union. If a widow has sons, she may elect to enter leviratic union because neither her sons nor her marriage cattle may accompany her if she returns to her father's or brother's homesteads. Rather than return alone to her parent or brother, to face the bleak prospect of not being able to remarry because she has married or grown sons, a woman may choose to live with her late husband's brother. She may also elect to live with a married son, or a mature unmarried son may build a homestead for her and support her.

If a widow has only given birth to daughters and is still within the child-bearing age, she may be less likely to accept leviratic union because her brother may wish her to return to his father's kraal, or his own kraal, bringing back with her the dowry cattle. A widow's senior brother assumes control over her dowry cattle until she marries again. He may even inherit his sister's dowry cattle in the event that she does not marry again.

A leviratic union with a deceased brother's wife offers certain economic and demographic advantages. By accepting his late brother's wife (or wives) a man gains control over her family herd and becomes a genitor of subsequent children. However, the property holdings of his deceased brother and his widows are kept in trust for the sons of the deceased. Also, from the standpoint of the late husband's lineage, his widow brought dowry cattle with her and demon-strated her ability to produce male offspring, a definite asset to her late hus-band's clan and lineage.

Leviratic unions among the Barabaig are optional arrangements for the continuance of a marriage affected by the death of a husband. In addition to considerations of economic, demographic, and social factors, a choice to enter into, or refuse, leviratic union may rest on knowledge of personality characteris-tics of the other individual. A brother may refuse to "inherit" his deceased brother's wife, whom he knows to be quarrelsome and a trouble maker, or a wife may refuse to be "inherited" by her late husband's brother, who may have a reputation for being brutal to his wives. Also, a first wife of a husband finds it difficult to accept a subordinate position to the wives of her deceased hus-band's brother. Not only will her hut be at the end of a line of huts, but her former number one ranking in a family hierarchy may become fourth or fifth in a leviratic union. Death of a husband does not logically bring a marriage to an end according to the Barabaig, but it seriously affects the various social align-ments of a considerable number of people. Through the institution of the levi-rate, marriage and property relations are preserved.

Death of a wife does not necessarily bring a marriage alliance between in-laws to an end. The institution of the sororate, in which an unmarried sister of the deceased wife may become the wife of her dead sister's husband, allows a marital union to continue. However, depending on the rank of the deceased wife, the sororate may or may not be seriously disruptive to domestic harmony in a polygynous household. An example of the sororate and its effect on domestic re-lations in a compound family is the case of Mudinangi.

Mudinangi was a man wealthy in wives, children and cattle. He had six wives, fifteen children, and several hundred head of cattle. At night, the cattle filled his large corral and his wives laughed musically as the children tumbled and ran around the huts. But a change was to take place that would turn this happy homestead into a place of bitterness.

Mudinangi's first wife died, leaving two daughters and a large herd of dowry cattle. Since the woman had not given birth to sons, there was a good possibility that her married brother would ask for the return of her dowry cattle. However, Mudinangi was a rich and politically influential man, belonging to one of the largest clans in Barabaig society, and the perpetuation of a marriage alliance was deemed highly desirable by the wife's brother. Therefore, Mudinangi was able to marry his deceased wife's younger unmarried sister. Through the institution of the sororate, the marriage and property relations between the two families were stabilized and preserved. No new bridewealth animal was given to the wife's brother and the dowry cattle of the dead woman served in the same capacity for her surviving sister. The new wife succeeded her dead sister to the rank of first or chief wife. After a few years, she gave birth to a son, who became *sid haraneg*, the legal heir to his father's cattle herd. Animosity grew between the sister of the deceased first wife and Mudinangi's second wife, who had for many years assumed that her own son, now a young man, would become her husband's heir. Tension and conflict grew between the two wives, each one accusing the other of foul deeds. Fearing for the health and safety of her baby, the chief wife accused the second wife of practicing sorcery and attempting to poison her child. Other wives took sides in the disputes and soon the homestead resembled a battleground with invisible lines drawn around the huts. Children grew suspicious of each other. In an attempt to restore harmony, Mudinangi built a second homestead a few miles away and moved his second wife and her co-wife allies to the new location. Although the sororate provided a stabilizing effect on the original marriage alliance, it proved to be highly disruptive when a substitute wife assumed the highest rank in the social structure of the family. Had the sororate been utilized to replace a deceased wife with junior standing in the family hierarchy, the possibility of internal conflict might have been avoided, or at least minimized.

Both the levirate and sororate are cultural solutions to the problem of preserving marital and property relations between the families of a husband and wife. Individual choice in activating a levirate or sororate is based on a number of contingencies and consequences, some of which are not fully perceived.

End of a Marriage

A Barabaig marriage ends in divorce for a number of reasons, depending upon the party initiating the action. Generally speaking, it is rare that a man will seek a divorce. Repeated adultery and constant quarreling of a wife are the major complaints of men. Sterility of the wife is not necessarily a good reason for a divorce because a Baraband may still value her companionship and good will. Besides, divorce of a childless wife means the return of her dowry cattle, which might seriously deplete the family herd. Economic considerations are always a part of every marriage and divorce arrangement. A marriage begins with a cattle transaction and usually ends in another cattle transaction.

Women seek divorce for different reasons than those advanced by men. Lack of economic support, with famine conditions in the homestead, is the chief reason for any woman to initiate divorce proceedings. A husband's refusal to send his wife to a ritual specialist in order to be cured of infertility or frequent miscarriages is the second major complaint of women wishing a divorce.

Initiating a divorce suit varies, depending upon whether it is the husband or wife who acts to obtain the divorce. A woman begins divorce proceedings by running away from her husband's kraal and going to live with her father or married brother. After she remains away for a few days, her husband usually follows her to enter into discussions with her parent or brother. He brings a small barrel of honey as a gift offering to his father-in-law or brother-in-law, hoping to placate him so that the discussions may proceed smoothly. After hearing separate versions of marital discord told by husband and wife, the wife's father or brother usually convince the girl to go back to her husband. On some occasions, a girl is forced to return to her husband against her will. In at least one instance, the forceful return of a runaway wife resulted in tragedy.

Utuw was living with her oldest married brother because her father had died before she could marry. Being of marriageable age, her brother Barahed had chosen a man for her to marry, but she had fallen in love with another man. Shortly after her wedding to the man chosen by her brother, Utuw ran away to join her lover. Barahed located her and brought her back to her husband. She ran away a second time only to be returned again under protest and much pleading. Barahed, who frequently beat his wives, could not understand his sister's objections to marriage to a brutal husband. After Utuw ran away a third time, Barahed, notified by her husband, became enraged and went out to find his sister. A short distance from his kraal, he found her hanging by a leather strap from a small tree. She had committed suicide rather than return to either her husband or her brother. Suicide being rare among the Barabaig, some elders accused Barahed of murdering his sister, but lack of evidence soon ended any possibility of legal action. Rumors persisted for a long time and, indeed, the story of Barahed and Utuw continues to be told and retold. It is a story with different messages for different people.

A man seeking a divorce from his wife follows a different procedure from that employed by the woman. In the presence of two elders of the neighborhood, a husband confronts his wife with his charges and reasons for wanting a divorce. He orders her to return to her father. Then, accompanied by the two elders, the husband goes to his wife's father's homestead and a series of councils are held. Sitting off to one side, the wife is allowed to testify on her behalf, but usually if the marriage problem has reached the council stage, divorce is almost a certainty. There remains only the discussion of marriage property, its ownership and transfer depending upon the existence or absence of children.

During British rule, a government sanctioned divorce was made available to the Barabaig by petitioning to a court, composed of tribal elders appointed and salaried by the government. For the payment of 7 shillings ($1.00 in U.S. currency) in court fees, it was possible to obtain a divorce without having to submit to the traditional Barabaig system of acquiring a divorce. The ease at which a government court divorce could be obtained through payment of a fee became an important factor in the rise of divorce rates among the Barabaig. Also, the role of the courts did not include the reconciliation of the husband and wife as part of its primary functions. Therefore, most cases dealing with marital problems ended in divorce being granted to a wife. The main problem the court had to deal with was the more complex one of the return of marriage cattle and their offspring which, since the inception of marriage, may have passed to different owners.

Having received either a traditional or "modern" divorce, a Barabaig woman is free to marry a man from a different clan than that of her former husband. After a woman has been married and divorced twice, she generally finds it difficult to marry again and instead becomes a concubine, *ghwarabastyand* or "Maker of fire," who may pass from one man to another.

7

Social Order

Pre-Colonial Times

Prior to the establishment of German colonial rule in 1891, Barabaig society was organized into a number of discrete, localized descent groups or clans called *doshing* (plural). Each clan or *dosht* was a territorially based community with an autonomous system of law and order for its residents. In response to raids by wide-ranging Masai warriors, all male members of a particular Barabaig clan built their homesteads in a defensive alignment with fences forming a long line of connected kraals. The outer gates were built to face different directions, but the inner gates were placed so that they provided access or exit routes from one kraal to another. In the same ward or district, a number of different clans engaged in fierce rivalry by comparing each others' tallies of Masai warriors killed in defense of their families, their cattle, and their land. Rivalry between certain Barabaig clans persists up to the present day and is basically a continuance of the pattern of rivalry formerly established when clans were localized descent groups and each vied for recognition of military prowess and superiority.

With the advent of German colonial administration, Masai warfare was reduced to small-scale cattle raids. Presumably, the pacification of the interior of what was to be called German East Africa produced changes in the ecological adjustment of the Barabaig and other tribes who were formerly the main targets of Masai military aggression. There is no question that under German and later British administration after 1918, the human and cattle populations increased greatly. This was due largely to the elimination of tribal warfare, the reduction of cattle-raiding, and the introduction of Western medicine in the treatment and prevention of certain human and livestock diseases. It is therefore likely that, given the conditions of human and cattle population expansion, territorial expansion was a necessary and logical corollary. In fact, Barabaig intrusion and settlement in neighboring tribal territories, such as the WaNyaturu and Wa-

Nyiramba, had been going on for a long time and presented problems for the British administration—problems that were never satisfactorily resolved and that continue to the present day.

Although there is common knowledge among the Barabaig that the cessation of Masai raids led to steady and rapid increase in livestock holdings, no consensus exists in explaining why territorial expansion necessarily had to result in fission and dispersion of localized descent groups rather than some form of drift or mass relocation in new territories. Accounts by several Barabaig elders who still remember their early youth in clan communities, indicate that a number of factors were responsible for the ultimate disperson of clans. While many elders agree that human and cattle population expansion were contributing factors to change in the pattern of residence, other conditions were cited as reasons for precipitating the dissolution of the clan community.

Formerly, the concentration of clan members within a local descent group or clan community required mechanisms for the reduction of in-group aggression among its members. One technique or solution that channeled aggression outward away from the clan was the institution of rivalry between clans, with raids and warfare conducted against neighboring tribes. Defense against Masai invaders also provided a means of promoting clan unity and social prominence through war honors. Raiding and warfare were outlets for any tensions generated through suppression of in-group hostility. With the imposition of colonial rule and the establishment of superordinate political systems, indigenous social control achieved by the clan system no longer performed its cohesive function. Elders say that in-group aggression (that is, physical violence) increased when out-group aggression was forbidden by the colonial government. Overcrowded living conditions brought about by human and cattle population increase were also cited as reasons for territorial expansion. Since the pacification of the interior now permitted territorial expansion under a colonial system of law and order physical mobility of clan members increased to a point where individual families, no longer requiring armed protection of their clansmen, separated from local clan groups and set up homesteads in new and formerly uninhabited areas. Whether psychological, economic, or political factors were responsible for providing the initial impetus for clan dispersion cannot be readily ascertained from the oral history of the Barabaig. For whatever historical event or events may have initiated clan fission, at the present time, all sixty-odd clans are dispersed throughout Barabaig territory and beyond.

The Clan

A clan or *dosht* is the largest political group in Barabaig society that is corporate in character, in that there is an acknowledged leader who inherits his office. Members claim descent from a common ancestral founder, and congregate on ritual occasions such as funerals to perform collective action. Cattle are considered as the legal property of the clan and bear distinctive clan brands by which they are identified.

Barabaig clans are part of a larger dual division that separates the tribe according to magico-religious functions. The two divisions are the *Daremgadyeg* (5 priestly or ritual clans) and the *Homat'k* (consisting of 55 laical or secular clans). Membership in a clan and clan division is determined by the patrilineal principle of tracing descent through the father and connecting male links up to a founding ancestor. While clan members are forbidden from marrying girls who are also clan members, there is no restriction to prevent members of one clan division from marrying someone from a different clan division, although male *Homat'k* prefer to marry a girl from one of the priestly or ritual clans.

Specialists from the *Daremgadyeg* clans offer their services when called upon to help promote human and cattle fertility. One clan in particular, the *Ghawog Mang*, perform rain-making rituals. Although a man is born into one of the ritual or priestly clans, it does not necessarily mean that he will perform any magico-religious service for his community. Individuals gain personal recognition as ritual specialists on the basis of their father's reputation and their own accomplishments.

Barabaig society includes two groups of specialists (the *Bisiyed*), a group of arrow-poison specialists who also perform circumcision operations, and the *Gidanwodik* (a clan of despised iron-smiths who furnish the Barabaig with iron spear blades, arrow points, branding irons, fleshing and scraping tools, and women's iron bracelets). Unlike other Barabaig clans, the *Bisiyed* and *Gidanwodik* only marry girls from within their own groups. Because of their occupational pursuits in handling what to the Barabaig is considered "dangerous" materials, the *Bisiyed* and especially the *Gidanwodik* are treated as social pariahs.

Barabaig clans vary in size from one family to several hundred members. Demographic differences in clan membership are due to a number of factors. Some clans have never fully recovered from the loss of members sustained during the Masai wars. Indeed, some clans were completely annihilated by the Masai. Other clans and their cattle survived the wars and cattle raids and increased in numbers until today they constitute some of the largest and wealthiest clans in all Barabaig society.

Many Barabaig men are able to trace their personal genealogies back seven to ten generations and up to the founding ancestor of their clans, although the order of succession in their genealogies may become confused when inquiry reaches beyond the fourth generation. A vertical "telescoping" of ancestors sometimes occurs, so a genealogy of ten generations in depth does not necessarily mean that the clan came into existence 250 years ago (assigning 25 years as a generation unit). Accuracy, therefore, in recounting genealogies is dependent upon memory recall and situational motivation of the individual members who comprise a clan.

All sixty-odd clans are identified by name, some of which are names of Barabaig founders, while others are terms to describe certain physical or behavioral characteristics (such as the way they plaster down their hair). Not all clans in Barabaig society were founded by Barabaig individuals. A number of clans were started by Masai aliens who reached Barabaig territory as migrants or war captives. Confusion and contradiction in accounts of the early history of

Barabaig clans indicate that oral history has either not been fully developed or it has since lost much of its former validating and legitimating functions.

Intraclan Relations

A Barabaig clan is subdivided socially, economically, and politically into a number of smaller groupings or lineages. A lineage can be visualized as a kind of demographic triangle in which the apex represents the male founder of the lineage and the area between the apex and the base includes all of his descendants, each of whom can actually trace the male connecting links between himself and the lineage founder.

Every Barabaig clan is subdivided into two or more *ga*, or what I will refer to as maximal lineages. These maximal lineages are ranked in order of seniority, following the social positions of wives and their sons in the ancestral polygynous household of the clan founder. Thus, for example, the senior maximal lineage of a clan having three maximal lineages (because the clan founder had three wives) is the group of members who trace their descent from the first son of the first wife of the clan founder. Intermediate ranking would be given to the maximal lineage that traces its genealogical connection to the first son of the second wife. The most junior maximal lineage is the grouping who are descendants of the first son of the third or last wife. In this way, ranking of lineages is determined by a combination of two principles—order of marriage of clan founder's wives and order of birth of sons to each wife.

A maximal lineage (*ga*) consists of a number of major lineages called *ghe*, which are also ranked according to the principles used to rank maximal lineages. Major lineages are generally no more than four generations in depth, which is the generational span between the great-grandfather and great-grandson. A six or seven generational span usually separates the great-grandfather from the founder of the maximal lineage. As the society moves through time, the four-generational span for a major lineage will be retained, but the personal names of the heads of junior major lineages will be forgotten and their descendants will identify with the senior major lineage founder. Through a process of lateral merging, names and positions in junior major lineages are eliminated.

A minor lineage consists of a grandfather with married sons who have male children. A married son with male children constitutes a minimal lineage, whether he is living within his father's homestead or in a separate residence.

Every male child must learn the Barabaig system of genealogical reckoning as part of his education and socialization in order to prepare him for the social, economic, and political life ahead. Mastering his personal genealogy, he will be able to orient his social behavior in face-to-face relations with other clan and lineage members in a culturally appropriate manner on the basis of his position in the genealogical structure of the clan. If he cannot do this, he is destined to commit social errors that may result in legal action being taken against him by an irate lineage or clan member. A social error committed against a lineage or clan member may cause him to be deprived of cattle from his herd.

If his cattle herd is to multiply in number, he must avoid becoming the recipient of a cattle fine imposed upon him by a fellow clansman.

When strangers meet it is necessary that they locate each other on some genealogical "map" before they can proceed to interact further in some social situation. To the question, "Gibandosh?" ("You are from which gate?") a stranger replies with the name of his clan. Inquiry will go no further if the men belong to different clans. If, however, they are clansmen, then the next question, "*Giba na ga?*" ("You are from which room?") is answered with the name of the maximal lineage. Having located the stranger genealogically, other information may now be exchanged without much hesitation. Of course, in clans with small memberships, all of the clansmen will be known, but in clans numbering several hundred it is possible not to know all of the members, especially children of clansmen.

Within every Barabaig clan there are a number of positions of ritual and political authority that are genealogically determined at various levels of segmentation. At the head of every maximal, major, minor, and minimal lineage there is an individual who exercises limited coercive power over the actions of his clan and lineage mates. He derives his senior ranking on the basis of being a lineal descendant in a senior genealogy (that is, the first son of the first wife of the first son and so forth) traceable to the family of the lineage or clan founder.

The *ashohoda dosht* or "clan head" is mainly a ritual functionary who presides over a group of clan elders during certain ritual gatherings such as funerals. In the past, when clans were localized communities, he may have held a position of absolute power. But with the dispersal of clan members throughout Barabaig territory, centralized clan leadership was superseded by leadership operating on neighborhood and ward or district levels.

At present, maintenance of clan integrity (such as legal enforcement of marriage rules prohibiting marriage of fellow clansmen and clanswomen) is the concern of senior clan members in different neighborhoods and wards. When word reaches a senior clan member that another clansman has violated certain clan norms or standards of conduct he confers with another senior member and together they may decide to hold a clan council or moot. A moot is a temporary gathering of senior clan elders with legal authority to sit in judgment and to impose punitive sanctions (such as cattle fines) on clansmen who have committed an offense against fellow clansmen or against the clan as a legal body. Legal decisions are arrived at through debate, the presentation of testimony, and final consensus on the part of senior elders who form a kind of jury, *makchamed* or "secret group," that renders a verdict. The offender is summoned to appear before the moot where he may present his version of the incident that led to his appearance before the group. There is no appeal of verdict from either clan or neighborhood moots, and the defendant invariably accepts the judgment of the moot and pays the customary fine of one bull and one cow.

Clan membership entails the acknowledgments of rights and the observance of obligations toward other members of one's clan. A clansman must stand ready to assist another clansman when his aid is solicited and, in turn, he expects future assistance from clansmen as part of his moral and legal rights.

If he is summoned to help carry a sick clansman on a litter to a mission or government hospital and he refuses, or if he declines to help move the homestead of a clan elder, his actions are considered breaches of clan norms and therefore punishable by moral and legal sanctions.

Rules of hospitality are norms that are part of the moral system involving clan membership. Their observance depends on the force of public opinion and reciprocity. A journeying clansman can almost completely rely on being fed and housed by fellow clansmen while en route to his destination. Refusal to show hospitality to fellow clansmen is almost inconceivable to the Barabaig.

Any show of physical violence between clansmen, short of homicide, is considered a serious breach in clan solidarity and is dealt with by the judicial system within the clan. Murder of a clansman or tribesman is viewed as a threat to tribal unity and falls under the jurisdiction of the tribal chief and tribal moot. Each clan has its own jural system, which may be activated in any neighborhood on any occasion requiring quick resolution of internal conflict between clansmen.

Conflict over inheritance cattle constitutes the greatest single trouble case brought before a clan moot. High incidence of litigation over inheritance cattle is not related to any ambiguity in rules of inheritance among the Barabaig, but is a consequence of the many cattle transactions made by the father during his lifetime. By far, the greatest difficulty of a legal heir to his father's cattle is to locate and return all of the milch cows loaned by his father to needy relatives. The case of Lakwai and Gidadelu contains most of the essential elements that comprise other cases involving disputes over inheritance cattle brought before clan moots.

Gidadelu was the legal heir of his father Gidamul, because he was the first-born son of Gidamul's second wife, the first wife having given birth to daughters but no sons. As Gidadelu grew up, married, and moved away, he always considered himself to be the sole heir to his father's herd. Indeed when his father prayed to God the name of Gidadelu was always mentioned. However, certain events occurred that were to change his status. After having given birth to daughters for a number of years, the father's first wife gave birth to a son, whom they named Lakwai. Now it was Lakwai who would be legal heir to his father's wealth. While Lakwai was still young, his father loaned six milch cows to Gidadelu because most of Gidadelu's livestock had been decimated by bovine pleuropneumonia. Shortly after, the father died of cerebral malaria and Lakwai was notified by his mother that six milch cows from the father's herd were in his brother's kraal. He had been too young at the time the milch cows were loaned to realize that they were part of his inheritance. Summoning Gidadelu to a meeting of clan members to decide on a funeral for the father, Lakwai confronted Gidadelu on the subject of the milch cows. Gidadelu denied that he ever received the cows and Lakwai then complained to his clan elders. Although the major lineage council had nearly reached agreement on a funeral for Gidamul, the constant bickering between Lakwai and Gidadelu resulted in the disruption of the meetings and a decision to abandon the idea of a funeral. Gidamul was exposed to the hyena, the final resting place for most Barabaig. A clan moot was convened and clan elders from adjacent neighborhoods arrived to help in the legal proceedings. In order to gather sufficient evidence to render a verdict, the clan elders delegated two young men to go to Gidadelu's herd to see if cattle fitting the description given by Lakwai's mother were among the animals. They reported back to the council and verified Lakwai's claim. Not only was Gidadelu directed to return the loan cows, which were rightfully part of Lakwai's inheritance, but Gidadelu was fined one bull and one cow for his duplicity. The bull and cow were brought before the council where the bull was killed, roasted, and eaten by all male clan elders attending the moot with the exception of Lakwai and members of his maximal lineage, who were customarily prohibited from eating an animal paid as a clan fine by a maximal lineage member. The cow became the property of Lakwai, a point that caused considerable bitterness in Gidadelu who now had another reason not to like Lakwai.

The existence of a moot system in Barabaig society effectively reduces the incidence of self-help as a means of counteraction and redress of grievances. Given the kind of ecological adjustment to physical environment achieved by the Barabaig, and given the social condition of clan disperson, the institution of a clan moot appears to be an effective form of social control, limited, however, to the regulation of behavior between clansmen.

Relations between Clans

Social and political relations between Barabaig clans as groups are minimal and usually involve individuals and their families, rather than their entire descent group. Formerly, an offense committed against an individual would involve all his clansmen who were morally and legally obligated to come to his aid. Retaliation by his clansmen against the offender would set off a counteraction and two clans would become involved in major conflict. Since there were no means of bringing together the two parties to the dispute, the conflict might escalate from a feud to a vendetta. Barabaig oral history contains an account of how a single murder of a member of the Hilbasalep clan led to the almost complete annihilation of the Hilbaghambomas clan in an interclan vendetta.

Ghambomas, who was the ancestral founder of what was later to become a clan, had brewed some honey-beer and invited Salep and his son to join him in a beer-drink. When Salep's son left to return home, he was killed by the son of Ghambomas for reasons that are obscure. Before Salep left, Ghambomas told him that if he encountered anything strange on his way home he should not be alarmed. Returning home on the same path by which he had come to the beer-drink Salep saw the body of his murdered son. On arrival at his homestead he told his sons and the mother of the dead son about the murder and told them not to grieve. Over a long period of time the sons of Salep married, had many sons who married, and the clan grew to a considerable size. One day all male clansmen received instructions that they must go and kill every male descendant of Ghambomas blood. They came to the fortification of Hilbaghambomas and, under cover of darkness, killed every male inhabitant except one member who, upon hearing of the massacre, went into hiding at his mother's clan stockade. Later, he had an opportunity to marry the daughter of a Hilbasalep clansman. After the birth of two male children, the father went to the Hilbasalep stockade and revealed his true identity. Rather than revive the former clan vendetta, amicable relations were established between the two clans.

While there is no way of vouching for the accuracy of the Hilbaghambomas-Hilbasalep historical account, the myth had such a profound influence on Gaseri, a former paramount chief of the Barabaig, that he decreed internecine warfare morally and legally reprehensible. He also decreed that it was punishable by a supernatural sanction called *gak* or "bones," a form of social pollution that affects not only the murderer but his sons and grandsons. Neither the murderer's wives nor children born before the murder are affected. But any male children born to the murderer after the crime inherit the *gak* from their father. *Gak*, therefore, is a supernatural sanction activated by the paramount chief on any occasion when a tribal member has killed another tribal member. In this way, self-help in the form of a vendetta by a particular clan against another clan is prevented and justice is served by a supernatural sanction. Aside from cases of murder of a fellow tribesman, any conflict between individuals belonging to different clans who do not share in-law relationships cannot be resolved by legal action.

The case of Mairu illustrates not only the lack of legal recourse in certain disputes between individuals of different clans, but also dramatically points out that among the Barabaig numerical superiority in clan membership also confers political supremacy in matters relating to settlement of grievances.

On May 5, 1959, Mairu joined a group of young men who went hunting for a lion which was seen in the neighborhood. A lion is considered an "enemy of the people." For killing a lion a man is rewarded by gifts of cattle by his relatives and social prestige which also enhances the status of his clan. When the group of men encountered the lion, Mairu was in position to throw the first spear. Although the spear did not kill the lion, the fact that it was the first spear to hit the lion entitled Mairu to claim credit for the kill. In his encounter with the charging lion, Mairu received severe lacerations on the chest and back from the claws of the enraged lion. By nightfall, word reached the newly established Lutheran mission at Balangda Lalu that a Barabaig boy had been badly mauled by a lion. Fortunately, the missionary and I were able to locate Mairu in the dark and to bring him back to the mission dispensary where his deep wounds were treated. He recovered, but credit for the lion kill went to a young man of the Daremgadyeg clan, one of the largest clans in Barabaig society. His spear had been the second one to hit the lion, but since he came from a very large clan and Mairu, who was not expected to live anyway, came from a clan numbering 20 males, Mairu was cheated out of his rightful claim to economic reward in the form of cattle and a lifetime of social prestige. Mairu had no legal recourse available to obtain redress and receive credit for the lion kill, so it became a closed incident. Traditionally, no legal action is available because there is no political articulation possible between individuals belonging to different clans. The size of the support group behind an individual determines whether or not he will attempt to claim rights usurped by individuals of other clans. Only in cases of murder will the paramount chief intervene and settle the trouble case by imposing a supernatural sanction on the murderer. Most of the politico-jural action necessary to resolve most disputes is taken care of by clan and neighborhood moots.

Being a Good Neighbor

Social interaction of people sharing the same geographic area (such as a neighborhood) are generally more intense and continuous than relations on either ward, district, or tribal level. Public affairs in the neighborhood, linked with conditions of drought, famine, disease, witchcraft, death, or noncooperative behavior of a fellow neighbor are generally managed by concerted action of the male elders. A neighborhood council may be convened by any local elder, who is then referred to as "mother of the council," for it is he who "gave birth" to the assemblage. Only male elders and young men may attend the meeting. Neighborhood councils are empowered to deliberate and judge only those matters which are of public concern for the neighborhood at large.

Transient residence linked with the cyclical growth and depletion of grazing areas does not permit the establishment of permanent leadership in any territorial group. In addition, the absence of any localized kin groups preclude the possibility of a clan or lineage forming the nucleus for a formal political structure with permanent authority. Although each Barabaig family and homestead is pursuing economic self-interest and advantage in terms of the welfare and increase of their own cattle herd, they are still reliant on group cooperation and effort in areas of noneconomic activity as well as in situations requiring common defense against disease, predatory animals, and cattle raids.

Shifting leadership is a characteristic feature of a Barabaig neighborhood council. Some elders are more skilled in oratory, better informed about judicial procedure and legal precedents, and possess certain personality characteristics that command respect. These individuals are given recognition as "spokesmen" and when they move away other "spokesmen" will emerge from the neighborhood, or move in from different neighborhoods.

Each neighborhood group is a separate ritual congregation with regard to the performance of collective ritual action. The intrusion of any element that cannot be tolerated or normally absorbed into the lives of the neighbors will be dealt with through collective deliberation and action. Any crisis affecting one homestead is thought of as affecting the entire neighborhood. In crises of sickness, disease, or when prophetic dreams tell of impending disaster the neighborhood council of men assembles to discuss the issue and arrive at some consensus about appropriate action. Precedent situations and cases are cited by elders while the younger men look on in silence. Some elders are noted for their memory, rhetoric, and perception and these men clearly dominate the discussions. A decision to temporarily isolate or quarantine the neighborhood initiates a series of rituals believed to have the power of "throwing off" the existing threat. A sheep is chosen as the sacrificial animal. It is suffocated in the prescribed ritual manner by stopping up its nostrils and preventing it from breathing through the mouth. No blood should be drawn while the animal is alive. After it is declared dead, strips of skin are taken from the sheep and hung on the larger trees surrounding the neighborhood. At the same time, the ritual brewing of honey-beer will complement and reinforce the effectiveness of the animal sacrifice and protective charms.

No stranger is allowed into any neighborhood holding a ritual designed to rid the place of a crisis. Any violation of this rule (which remains in effect for two days) reduces the effectiveness of the rituals and is therefore considered a public offense. A fine of honey is levied not against the stranger, but against the neighbor who may be responsible for the stranger's presence and violation of their quarantine.

Neighborhood councils have the power to invoke negative sanctions, ranging from a fine of honey to banishment from the community and a death curse. Failure on the part of an adult male to participate in councils or unwillingness to render assistance in communal action is subject to fine. Although the neighborhood council or moot cannot assess a fine of cattle, if the offense is serious (such as witchcraft) the group can render a magical sanction against the accused to force his confession and departure from the community. A litter similar to the one used in carrying a human corpse away is built, thus symbolizing the death of the accused. This death curse, called *moshtaid*, is generally effective in extracting a confession from the alleged witch, who soon leaves the neighborhood and goes to live where his reputation for witchcraft is unknown.

Relations between the Sexes

Regulation of social relations between the sexes appears to be largely the prerogative of women. Women, collectively and individually, hold certain rights, the infringement of which leads to a spontaneous reaction from the women in the neighborhood in which the offense occurred. The legal status of Barabaig women is reflected in the jural institution of *girgwaged gademg*, "council of women," a moot composed of neighborhood women elders who collectively act and deliberate as a judicial body, passing judgment on men who have violated certain of their rights. Their ability to fine men for infringement of their rights is validated by myth and actualized by communal opinion and actions of the women. Women's rights and their power to fine men derives from a myth that tells of a promiscuous state of men and women before the institution of marriage was created by Udameselgwa, a female deity held in high reverence by Barabaig women.

> Long ago, in the beginning of time, women had no husbands but moved about from kraal to kraal, staying only a short time with each man. When they gave birth, the sons stayed with the fathers while the daughters moved on with their mothers. Men did all of the cattle-herding, milking, and cooking. One day, tired of their inferior status, the women went to a powerful female magician, named Udameselgwa

and asked her to help them. She gave them a magical potion and instructed them how to use it, assuring them that it would affect the minds of men.

One day, after a heavy rain, the men returned home after herding their cattle. They were cold and wet and noticed that the women had made the fires. Secretly, the women had sprinkled some of the magical potion into the fires. The men sat huddled near the fires and their warmth, combined with the potion, made them reluctant to leave the fires. They told the women to go out and milk the cows. While milking the cows, the women put the magical potion into the milk gourds and gave them to the men. Upon drinking the milk, the men's minds began to change. That night, each woman stayed with the man she was with at the time and continued to stay. This was the beginning of marriage. Hereafter, the men were afraid of losing the women and began to respond to their wishes.

The high social status of Barabaig women may be linked to their important ritual contributions. Certain magico-religious rituals are carried out exclusively by women. In their singing of religious "hymns" to solicit aid from God, *Aset,* by communicating with the spirits of deceased "priests" from ritual clans, intermediaries between God and the living, the women display a ritual competence acknowledged by the men as essential for the general welfare of the society in times of disease, famine, and drought.

When a Barabaig woman believes that one or more men in the neighborhood have committed an offense against her by violating certain rights of women she complains to other women who decide informally whether or not to convene a moot. An offense committed against one woman is seen as an offense committed against all women, thus inciting the female elders of the community in which the offense occurred to seek redress by jural retaliation. Between the men and women of the neighborhood there develops a feeling of antagonism, but for different reasons, the sentiments of the women being offended because their rights have been violated by a man, and the sentiments of the men aroused because the women will deprive a man of property by imposing a cattle fine. The disgruntled state of men is manifested in the oft-repeated phase, "They (the women) are going to 'eat' (consume) cattle needlessly."

Much of the women's jural procedure is strikingly similar to the pattern of behavior exhibited by the men during their councils. The council place is usually under a shade tree previously selected by some of the council members. Every day during the course of the trial, which may last from three to six days, the women leave their homesteads and gather under the shade tree. Deliberations begin in the late morning and last until late afternoon, at which time the women disperse and return to their homesteads to cook the evening meal. It is obligatory for all married women of the neighborhood to attend the meetings. Exemptions are made in cases of sickness, child care, and herding duties.

The male offender may be present to explain and defend his actions, but sometimes a man chooses to avoid risking further antagonism and does not attend. In any event, the opportunity to challenge the allegations of women is available to those who would choose to debate the issue. Sometimes the moot is prolonged by internal dissension. Wives, female members of the defendant's clan, and friends may try to defend the transgressor, even when they realize that an unfavorable verdict is inevitable. Precedents and parallels between the present offense and offenses punished in the past are cited by knowledgeable older women in the group. Certain precedents may not be known or remembered by the women who comprise a particular moot and therefore deliberation may be more difficult. Still, there is a body of common knowledge which refers to some of the offenses which have, in the past, evoked the sanction called *ghordyod gademg*, "fine of the women."

Women's rights are embodied in certain basic concepts or postulates concerning the sanctity of the female body and domestic harmony during the critical period of childbirth, which when challenged or threatened incites legal action on the part of neighborhood women. Some of the offenses that are liable to prosecution are the following:

If a husband kicks his wife's cooking stones, his action implies a wish for her death.

If a husband beats his wife after she returns from a *werwerik*, a neighborhood mission of sympathy for a woman who has just given birth.

If the midwife hears the husband beating another wife during the time when his pregnant wife is about to give birth.

If a husband beats his wife during her one-month convalescence after childbirth, the period called *ghereg*.

If the husband swears at the midwife while she is still performing her duties, or if he wishes to send her away before her customary period of attendance has lapsed.

If the husband hits his wife over the head with his stick.

If the husband takes away his wife's clothes and sends her away from the homestead in a naked condition.

If any man, including the husband, witnesses a childbirth.

If a goat, sheep, or bullock is solicited from a male neighbor in order to provide food for a convalescent mother and the man refuses to contribute the animal.

If a man rapes a prepubescent girl.

If a man ill-treats a sexually amoral girl by physical abuse.

Gesturing and oratory of female elders standing before the women's council closely resembles the actions of male speakers at their meetings. A woman addresses her remarks to a "receiver," a woman selected by the speaker to reinforce her verbal delivery from time to time by assenting and repeating certain key words of the oration, thus lending emphasis to the speaker's pleading. The speaker strikes the ground with her stick or swings it around while exhorting the audience, who respond with a chorused shout of approval. She may modulate her voice from a barely audible level until it rises gradually to emotional shouting, grimacing, and expressions of anger and disgust. However, for the most part, the jural proceedings are conducted with a moderate display of emotion.

The women's council, usually numbering about 50 women, is an "open" meeting in the sense that any married woman may have the opportunity to speak before the group and, unlike male councils that exclude women, the women permit men to attend the moot. A few men, usually fewer than ten in number, sit apart from the women's group but within hearing distance of the proceedings. Neighborhood men may try to defend their accused neighbor by pitting their oratorical skills against female protagonists, but rarely are moot decisions reversed because of the intervention of neighborhood men. Some men take the opportunity to chide and rebuke the women about "unjust" decisions in the past. The obstructive tactics of the men appear to be aimed at defending the accused man and, at the same time, disparaging and discrediting the jural institution of the women. Men complain bitterly about the existence of women's councils and often voice their wishes for abolition of these moots. However, dissension among men has not yet generated organized opposition on a large scale.

During the council proceedings, numerous deviations from the objectives of the moot occur frequently and appear to be beyond the control of women informally recognized as "spokesmen." The occasion of a moot provides an opportunity to air a wide variety of grievances concerning such things as a husband's sale of part of his wife's dowry cattle, child welfare, and the iniquities of men in general, as well as the one on trial.

A women's council never ends in an acquittal for the defendant, although women's decisions pertaining to the sanction may be modified because of circumstances surrounding the defendant. If a man with a small herd of cattle is unable to pay the cattle fine, one young black bull, the women may consider a fine of several gallons of raw honey as indemnification. The honey is then consumed on the spot by the women. A man with "gak," the ritual condition of pollution because he is a murderer or son of a murderer, will also be fined honey instead of cattle. The rationale for this action may be seen in the sacred nature of honey and the profane character of the man's cattle. Whereas the women fear eating any meat of an animal belonging to a man with "gak" for fear of becoming contaminated, the eating of honey is permissible, since honey is considered sacred and is not capable of being contaminated by a man who is ritually unclean.

When the defendant learns that the women's council has adjudged him guilty of having violated women's rights, he must send a young black bull to a spot where it will be beaten to death with sticks. Beating of the bull by the women may be symbolic of what they would like to do to the man, but instead inflict punishment and death on his surrogate.

Until the moment when the cattle fine is paid, neighborhood men will actively try to dissuade the women from carrying out their decision. Men place themselves between the advancing group of women and the bullock being brought by the defendant or his assistant. They try to obstruct the passage of the women, but the women drive them away by threatening to hit them with their sticks. The action of blockage and the pleading of the men does not usually alter the course of legal action of the women. They have made up their minds to collect the fine.

Not all women present in the council are permitted to hit the bullock over the head with their sticks. Only those women who are married to a man be-

Women's council going to collect cattle fine.

longing to the same generation as the male offender are considered eligible to beat the bullock. Also, no woman who is a member of the same clan as the offender would consider killing an animal belonging to her own clan.

After the eligible women hit the bullock, but usually without killing it, some men assist the women by tossing the bullock to the ground and suffocating it by stopping up its nostrils and tying a leather thong around its jaws. After the bullock is dead, each woman of the council is permitted to touch the carcass with her herding-stick and later the meat of the dead animal will be divided among the women, first choice of portions going to the women who comprised the eligible group that first administered the beating.

One case is illustrative of a rare situation in which a man refused to comply with the decision of the women's council and challenged their authority to impose a cattle fine. In 1955, Ghutadyonda was away from his homestead when a bullock was taken from his herd and killed to provide food for a convalescent mother in the neighborhood. Ghutadyonda encountered the women skinning his bull and became so angry that he threw a spear at them to chase them away. The women convened a moot and fined Ghutadyonda, who refused to pay the cattle fine. His refusal brought in action the women's sanction of *gibuhand*, a devastating fine and death curse. The women tore down his kraal fence and returned his wives back to their fathers. They went into the huts of the wives and threw the ashes from the hearths onto the beds and scattered the emainder around the room, all the while making mourning cries to symbolize hat a death had occurred in the homestead—Ghutadyonda's death.

For one year, Ghutadyonda's relatives pleaded with the women of the neighborhood to reconsider their action. A moot was convened and it was decided that before Ghutadyonda's wives could be returned to him, and the curse of death removed, Ghutadyonda would have to pay a fine of two black bullocks and would have to brew honey-beer to take away the death curse they had imposed on him. This time, he recognized the jural authority of the women and complied with their decree. Social relations were again restored between Ghutadyonda and the women of the neighborhood.

Although the women's council is convened presumably to help restore harmony in social relations between the sexes in the neighborhood, some women discussants manifest strong feelings of antagonism toward men in general. Expressions of ridicule and contempt comprise part of the tangential and inappropriate discussions which emerge during the judicial proceedings.

There are other social contexts in which women display antagonism toward Barabaig men. During a wedding, neighborhood women engage in the special song and dance called *dumd dumod*, "dance of the penis," in which a singing rivalry emerges between women who boast of their sexual prowess in vanquishing the men of their husbands' clans. The presence of ritual obscenity and ridicule during a wedding reception is only one indication of sexual antagonism manifested by women toward men. Another part of the wedding ritual consists of a mime play in which one woman, acting the role of "husband," is deceived and made to look ridiculous by a second woman playing the part of the "new wife" cooking her first meal for her husband. The female spectators howl with delight over the antics of the two performers, but none of the men present in the homestead cares to see either the play or to see and hear the lewd dancing and singing of the *dumd dumod*.

Another occasion when antagonism between the sexes is manifested in ritual behavior occurs during a séance. Although the audience at a séance is mixed, women spectators considerably outnumber the men. The medium, who is always a woman, elicits the spirit of a man named Gidamagir, who proceeds to vilify and harass the women attending the séance. According to myth, Gidamagir's hostility toward women originates from the time women refused to pull out an arrow from his body when he returned from battle with a tribal enemy. He finally located a small boy who succeeded in extracting the arrow, but Gidamagir died shortly after. It is believed that to this day his spirit continues to rebuke and deprecate women for their refusal of aid that would have saved his life. Shortly after Gidamagir's bitter and violent denunciation of women, the spirit of Udameselgwa, the female deity, intercedes on behalf of the women and is heard quarreling with Gidamagir until both spirit voices fade away. The rest of the séance is devoted to the elicitation of spirits of deceased priests who answer questions concerning personal problems put to them by the audience.

The women's council, *girgwaged gademg*, operates as part of the legal machinery that goes into action to mend a breach in neighborhood relations caused by an offense committed against a female member of the community, and its potential threat covertly regulates the day-to-day relations between the sexes in the neighborhood. It also functions to preserve the relatively high social and legal status of Barabaig women. The redressive mechanism of *girgwaged gademg* is a unique cultural phenomenon that does not exist among any of the related Eastern Sudanic groups to which the Barabaig belong, nor does mention of women's councils empowered to impose punitive sanctions against men appear in literature dealing with other African societies.

The Political Field

Barabaig tribal territory has always been considered to be a "trouble area"—first by the German colonial administration, then the British, and now the independent government of Tanzania. The Barabaig were never a docile people, resisting to the death any invasion or threat to themselves, their cattle herds, and their territorial sovereignty. When the Masai, the most war-like and feared of the East African tribes, invaded Barabaig territory, they were met with strong resistance from Barabaig warriors, with high death toll on both sides. Some ravines and plains still carry the names of these battles. As long as the technology of war on both sides was roughtly comparable, there was a general "stand-off," with neither side clearly the victor.

In the years prior to 1884–1885, the dates of the Berlin Conference, there was a "scramble for Africa" in which a number of European governments attempted to lay claim to territory in Africa. In East Africa, the major European powers involved in the struggle for land annexation were the Germans, the British, and the Portuguese. The Berlin Conference established the "ground rules" under which a territory could be claimed by a European government and the partitioning of Africa into colonial territories was begun. Barabaig territory fell under German colonial rule but it was some time before a German military expedition actually entered their land.

From the turn of the century, the Germans began building numerous concrete and adobe fortifications linking the remote areas of their new colony of German East Africa with the colonial administrative centers at Tanga and Dar es Salaam. No forts were built in Barabaig territory, but the closest forts at Mbulu, Singida, and Mkalama were within three or four days march of any part of Barabaig territory. Shops run by Arabs, Somalis, and later Indians, sprang up around the forts and new towns appeared, supported by the revenue gained from supplying the colonial garrison stationed there. Being located in remote and semiarid regions, these towns and surrounding areas had little appeal for European settlers. In turn, the absence of a European settler population meant that any European influence on Barabaig culture would be limited to actions on the part of the German garrison. European colonial personnel stayed in or close to the forts, going out occasionally on patrol. Interest in what the British were doing in nearby Kenya Colony was higher than that regarding the development of the interior of the northern districts.

A few dirt roads running roughly north-east by south-west were cut through Barabaig territory, mostly by neighboring horticulturalists and a few Barabaig pressed into service. But the Barabaig were generally considered to be "useless" in their handling of iron hoes in digging and levelling the dirt roads. They ran away and moved their homesteads whenever they heard that labor recruiting or conscription was taking place nearby. With their ease of physical mobility, the Barabaig successfully avoided much work on roads, which had no value or utility for their way of life.

Political resistance against the Germans continued to be advocated by prophets and war-leaders, mostly the Badyut subtribe of Datog and the Aradyik clan of the Barabaig. In an effort to put down the mounting resistance to German colonial rule, two military expeditions from the forts at Mbulu and Singida rounded up a dozen or more prophets and clan leaders and hanged them in public view as a demonstration of colonial power. The bodies were allowed to hang for days so that all who believed in the power of the prophets would be convinced of the superiority of German colonial rule. These public executions successfully crushed the spirit of open resistance of the Barabaig and sent the remaining traditional leaders into secret residence. They continued to operate incognito, being referred to by different names for so many years that the later administration of the British believed the Barabaig to be without a chief or any form of traditional leadership. It thus set about to appoint a number of Barabaig elders to the newly-created positions of tribal chief, sub chiefs, and headmen, who would implement governmental policy at the tribal, county, and ward levels, respectively.

Barabaig territory continued to be a troubled or politically sensitive area and British administration operated with minimal influence. Poll and cattle head taxes were imposed on Barabaig cattle-owners by the government and collected by the salaried chief, subchiefs, and headmen. Unlike other areas of Tanganyika, where the imposition of taxes forced a large part of the adult male population to migrate to the cities to work as wage laborers, any Barabaig tax-payer could sell one of his animals at a local cattle auction and receive enough money to pay his taxes and have no need to leave Barabaig territory for any monetary purpose.

Most of the Barabaig employed as government agents spoke little or no Ki-Swahili, the colonial administrative language and lingua franca of East Africa, and no British officials spoke the Barabaig language. The result was that communications between government officials and their Barabaig agents and the Barabaig masses were barely possible. To correct these conditions in the future, a number of schools (both missionary and government run) were established in different parts of the territory. Elders informally learned Ki-Swahili in conversation around trading settlements that sprang up at certain points along the dirt roads. The rest they learned from their children attending school, although the number of children actually in school was very small.

Barabaig resistance to cultural innovations planned for them by the Tanganyika government led the government to adopt stronger measures against the recalcitrant stand of Barabaig elders. Each family was to provide one student for the local school and these reluctant scholars were rounded up by the headman of each ward. Children in the least desirable social and economic position in a family were selected by their father to attend school. School attendance was very poor, with many children constantly running away or too sick to attend. Headmen were constantly returning runaway school children and their fathers protested when they had to pay fines for having runaway children. During a cattle auction, when taxes, fines, and school fees were collected, fathers even grumbled when they had to pay their children's annual school fees—42 shillings ($6.00 U.S. currency) tuition and board per child and 27 shillings ($4.00) if the child lived within walking distance of the school. For selling a medium-sized animal at the cattle auction, a man received approximately 145 shillings ($20.00). When circumcision ceremonies were about to take place near the school area, scores of schoolboys would be locked up in tiny rooms to prevent them from running away to join the boys to be circumcised. Strong resentment bordering on revolt was stirred up when boys who managed to run away from school were forced to return, sometimes when the ritual had already begun.

In spite of the conditions under which formal western-type education was introduced, many boys and girls managed to complete at least two or three years of schooling, but returned to herding cattle for lack of any opportunity to put their new-found literacy to use. Most Barabaig did not take advantage of the bus services appearing more frequently along their dirt roads. And very few Barabaig, usually sons of poor families, went outside the territory to work. The outside world was a place full of danger, as everyone knew from experience with the Masai, the Germans, and the British.

Candidates for the position of tribal chief were selected on the basis of literacy and fluency in Ki-Swahili and membership and political influence in larger clans. Some government-appointed chiefs lasted less than one year in office, being either incompetent, corrupt, or ineffectual in their dealings with their own people. Autocratic chiefs lasted longer, sometimes a decade, but they were no more successful in bringing the rest of the Barabaig into closer harmony or to acceptance of Western culture (British style) than their short-termed predecessors. British administrators (the district commissioners and district officers) were assigned to new posts periodically and never reached an understanding of Barabaig life and culture. They spent most of their time in and around the forts and towns, making only one- or two-day trips to the Barabaig during their monthly or bimonthly inspection tours of their district. Sometimes, Barabaig young men threw spears at the tires of their vehicles. Most Barabaig, however, avoided contact with representatives of the government, including their own Barabaig agents. For the Barabaig, the government of Tanganyika was as the present government of Tanzania is—a remote entity existing beyond the horizon, as mysterious and dangerous as the land itself.

Powers of the traditional chief or ŋutamid were curtailed when his capacity to initiate and direct war parties and cattle raids was removed through the imposition of a British system of law and order. Throughout the period of British rule, the traditional chief continued to exercise certain powers in authorizing circumcision and funeral ceremonies. He presided over a council of elders, girgwaged getabarak or "council of the wide tree," convened to impose sanctions against nyone who was insubordinate to him, had killed a fellow Barabaig, or had ought with another man during a circumcision or funeral ceremony. Being lliterate and not knowledgeable in Ki-Swahili and the ways of European government and culture, he could not use his political position to influence governmental policy toward the Barabaig. He neither understood the new problems reated by government and cultural change in Tanganyika, nor possessed the recessary skills to find and effect adequate solutions to these new problems. He remained in the background, ever watchful over the actions of the government-appointed chief and his associates.

Antagonisms developed between the government-appointed chief and the raditional chief whenever the appointed chief tried to extend his sphere of jurisdiction and influence into Barabaig traditional life. On occasion, circumvention of the traditional political system by the government-appointed chief brought quick reprisal from the traditional chief. Traditional and mandated political systems were two separate systems with different spheres of jurisdiction and different sets of rights and obligations regarding the exercise of social control over their subjects. Erosion of traditional political authority continued slowly and inexorably, with certain incidents revealing the boundaries of power between the two protagonists. The case of Gitamuk, the government-appointed chief, is illustrative of cultural and political change among the Barabaig in its simplest form.

In 1955, a funeral or *bunged* for a deceased member of the Daremgadyeg clan was held without the authorization of the traditional chief, who was neither notified nor invited to attend. A council of tribal elders was convened by the traditional chief and they decided to put the eldest son of the deceased's first wife in social isolation or *radod*, a sanction that includes the recall of a man's wives by their fathers, quarantine of his homestead, and avoidance of social contact and communication with the person. Gitamuk, the government-appointed chief, being a member of the same clan as the man fined, advised his clansmen to ignore the sanction of *radod* and ordered the funeral to proceed. This interference and subversion of traditional authority so infuriated the traditional chief that he threatened to refuse permission to hold any funerals or circumcision celebrations, especially those of the Daremgadyeg clan and clans belonging to the Daremgadyeg division.

After a one-month delay in the Daremgadyeg funeral, the man in *radod* sent an appeal to the traditional chief to remove his social isolation by re-convening the tribal council. *Radod* can only be lifted by having a second sanction imposed on a man by the *girgwaged getabarak*, "council of the wide tree," the tribal council of elders. Meeting to consider the appeal, the traditional chief and council elders decided to impose a cattle fine, *njagod*, consisting of one bull to be paid to each leader of the four oldest clans in Barabaig society—the Aradyik, Halamg, Sedoyek, and Hilbagrangai. Having paid the cattle fine, the son of the deceased man was allowed to continue his father's funeral.

The power struggle between Gitamuk, the government-appointed chief, and the traditional chief continued and several months later, at another funeral, they met in face-to-face confrontation and bitter debate. Angered by Gitamuk's continuing challenge to his authority, the traditional chief threatened to ban all funerals in the future. Some of the elders attending the funeral were also members of the government-appointed tribal council and, worried that the chief would carry out his threat to ban all funerals, met in secret session and decided to take action to remove Gitamuk from his office of tribal chief. Recommendations for dismissal of Gitamuk as tribal chief were submitted to the British administration. One month later, Gitamuk was removed from political office—his challenge and subversion of traditional political authority being his political downfall.

Traditional political authority, in the form of a paramount chief, ŋ*utamid*, is legitimated by mythological validation and possession of supernatural power since he is the possessor of the *gadyak't*, a magic fire used as war magic against other tribes in the days prior to the advent of German rule. Succession to the office of paramount chief is determined patrilineally, from father to son, within a maximal lineage of the Aradyik clan, one of the oldest, largest, and wealthiest clans in Barabaig society.

Although the power of traditional chief has diminished continuously during German and British rule, he still holds the traditional symbols of political legitimacy and gains compliance support from the masses, his office being the only traditional "bridge" between Barabaig clans and lineages. Together with the family councils, neighborhood councils, lineage and clan councils, the traditional chief and his tribal council of elders have maintained traditional Barabaig law and order in the face of opposition and change introduced by two European-type governments and the independent government of Tanzania.

8

The Problem of Death

Explanations of Death

DEATH AND DISEASE are two facts of life that every Baraband recognizes at a very early age. He is surrounded by the dead, the dying, and the sick. During disease epidemics, the sounds of wailing women fill every neighborhood in a seemingly endless fugue. Whooping cough, small-pox, meningitis, and occasionally bubonic plague, decimate the population and leave the survivors with innumerable, unanswered questions. "Why did my child die?" "Who could do this to me?" In the absence of a germ theory of disease causation, the Barabaig search for explanations to fit their conception of the world around them.

The Barabaig recognize symptoms of a number of diseases and have in their language specific terms to identify and discuss these disease states or conditions. Traditional medical practices exist to counteract the symptoms. If a man has a pain in the chest or back, a glowing stick from the fire is placed on the spot where the pain resides. Young and old alike carry the scars of countless applications of *bast* or "fire." Hardly any part of the body is spared the treatment. Symptoms of pleurisy are treated by swallowing a mixture made from arrow poison. For mumps, a magical grass vine is worn around the neck. Smooth pebbles from the stomach of an ostrich are placed in a small leather pouch and worn around the arm or neck as a protective charm to "throw off" disease. All of these precautions and treatments are directed at an invisible force projected upon the people by sorcery, witchcraft, vengeful ancestral spirits, or an angry God. From the vast panorama of death and disease, beliefs and explanations intertwine and reinforce each other.

Genesis of a Witch

A witch is a person whose physical presence is enough to cause a calamity. Witches, both male and female, are identifiable by the tragic stream of events they leave in their wake. If a man gazes at someone else's cattle herd and shortly after an animal gets sick and dies, he is accused of possessing an evil eye. A neighborhood council of elders meet and impose a death curse to drive him from the neighborhood. Sometimes, a series of events involving the same person in time and space are interpreted as proof of the person's inherent and malevolent power.

Udabasod, childless, and the only wife of Gisiged, was passing a crater lake where she noticed a dog drinking deeply from the water. She remarked to the dog's owner, "If this dog were a gourd, it would hold enough water to supply a homestead for a month." Next day, the dog's belly began to swell and, shortly after, the dog died. The childless couple continued to live in the neighborhood but another incident marked the end of their residence. While watching a group of children who were trying to stand on their hands, Udabasod noticed one very agile child who could stand for a long time on his hands, with both feet in the air. Udabasod predicted, "If this child grows up, he will be an expert dancer." This remark was heard by the boy's mother who was standing nearby. In the evening, the boy developed a fever and died suddenly. His mother remembered the remarks of Udabasod and told her husband, Gidamuidaghat, who became angry and summoned neighborhood elders to a council. They concurred that Udabasod was a witch and must be punished. Gisiged, Udabasod's husband, upon hearing that a neighborhood council had convened to discuss the witchcraft of his wife, packed his few belongings, his spear, milk gourds, skin bed, and with his wife and cattle herd abandoned his homestead and moved to another neighborhood where he hoped news of his wife's reputation would not reach. He chose flight rather than face the angry accusations and dangerous oath-taking of his neighbors.

Sorcery and Its Detection

Puzzling events that occur suddenly or persist for a long time are explained as being due to human or supernatural causation or a combination of both. Whereas a witch may cause certain events to occur by spoken words or mere presence, a sorcerer must employ certain material objects in a clandestine manner to achieve desired results. Although the Barabaig do not make fine distinctions between witchcraft and sorcery in terms of the presence or absence of human volition or intention, they nevertheless recognize certain signs (such as a prolonged run of bad luck or two deaths in a single homestead) as being due to the practice of sorcery, anger of ancestral spirits, or a punitive God. Witchcraft is suspected when single events occur in different homesteads in a neighborhood, whereas sorcery is manifested in a continuous series of misfortune, sickness, and death to people and livestock in a particular homestead of a neighborhood where no other homestead is similarly affected. If a solitary hyena is seen running around the neighborhood for a number of nights, witchcraft is believed responsible for the sufferings experienced in a number of neighborhood kraals. Witches are known to be capable of transforming themselves into hyena and can travel great distances.

Where doubt exists concerning the interpretation of certain signs as being either manifestations of witchcraft or sorcery, a Baraband can consult a diviner, *sitetehid*, who, by picking up stones five times with his right hand and looking at the pattern of the remaining pile of stones on the ground, can diagnose the cause of a person's trouble. For a cure to the problem diagnosed by the diviner, a man will have to go to a *daremgadyand*, a ritual specialist or priest. If the cause has been diagnosed as spirit vengeance, the troubled man may summon one of the traveling mediums, usually a woman, who, by contacting her familiar spirit while under self-induced trance, may transmit a message from the client's ancestral spirits telling him why they are angry. Provided with information that an ancestral spirit is angry because his kin have neglected him, a man can now take ritual action to correct his misfortune. He brews a pot of honey-beer, the sacred drink, and invites two old men (believed to be already close to becoming ancestral spirits themselves) to a beer-drink. Some of the honey-beer is poured on the ground in the living space, *samod*, and the cattle corral. Two young men are delegated to bring a gourd of honey-beer to the funerary monument or sacred grove of the dead ancestor who it is believed has been "throwing" misfortune on the man's homestead. After propitiating the dead ancestor by pouring the honey-beer into a hole in the side of the earthen monument (or around the sacred grove if the earthen monument no longer exists) the young men report back to the troubled homestead owner and everyone waits to observe the effects of their ritual actions. If death or sickness continues to trouble the homestead, the only remaining solution is to move the household and cattle herd to a new neighborhood.

Strange or deviant behavior in a person not labeled a witch is believed to be the work of a sorcerer bent on changing the person's mind. People are said to be victims of sorcery when they wander about repeating names or mistakenly believe that someone's herd or homestead is their own. Women have sexual hallucinations and some women constantly refer to their vagina while in conversation with others. In other ways, they are considered rational and are allowed to cook, to bear children, and to work, but not to herd livestock. Some young girls think they are men and carry spears or climb trees, acts that are normally appropriate to men.

Hallucinations and deliriums in political rivals near death are believed to be effects of some potion concocted by a sorcerer. In 1959, the government-appointed chief of the Barabaig died suddenly under mysterious circumstances. A short time later, a political aspirant to the traditional title of paramount chief, ŋutamid, died of what the Barabaig believed to be sorcery, but was actually syphilis of the brain. Next, the traditional chief of the Barabaig was brought to a mission hospital suffering from some unknown malady. Based on knowledge of relations between the three men, Barabaig elders speculated that both the government-appointed chief and the bitter rival of the traditional chief were victims of sorcery contracted for by the traditional chief. After the death of the lineage rival for the paramountcy, the traditional paramount chief became gravely ill as a result of counter-sorcery emanating from kinsmen of the dead lineage rival who were avenging his death. How else could the Barabaig explain the symptoms of delirium in all three persons, the deaths of a chief and a political aspirant, and the near-death of the traditional chief, all within a short period of time?

Death of an Elder

Not all deaths are considered by the Barabaig to be unnatural events. Elders past 45 or 50 years of age are believed to die of old age when their death is not sudden or surrounded by an aura of mystery or puzzling circumstances. However, the death of every Barabaig man, woman, and child must be discussed by a council of neighborhood men before deciding on the disposal of the body. Most women and all children who die are placed out in the surrounding bush where they are consumed by the hyena. Only certain male and female elders will be destined to receive a burial, but these individuals must have led exemplary lives or have been parents of numerous children. Other qualifications include the possession of sufficient wealth by married sons to buy honey with which to brew large quantities of honey-beer to be consumed at various stages of the eight- or nine-month long funeral.

A *bunged*, funeral, is the most significant and elaborate ritual in Barabaig society. It is singular in the size of its ritual congregation, the length of its performance, and the expenditure of wealth and cooperative effort necessary for a memorable and, indeed, historic event. Years are not numbered by the Barabaig, but remembered and referred to by certain events, such as "year of bubonic plague," "year of locusts," and years identified as "year of Giloma's funeral," "year of Gambul's funeral," and so forth. Social prestige accrues to the clan of the deceased whose funeral is so successful that it serves as a reference point in the Barabaig conception of time.

Decision to hold a *bunged* for a deceased male elder is normally made by a council composed of the deceased's married sons and their lineage and clan members living in adjacent neighborhoods. If the deceased was a member of a small clan, whose members are not wealthy in cattle, a funeral is almost an impossibility since it is as much a clan affair as it is a family observance. Indeed, the reputation of a clan is at stake if the funeral of a clansman does not proceed smoothly or if certain norms associated with various procedures and rituals are not adhered to. Unless the correct performance of a *bunged* can be assured, the entire project will be abandoned.

Deliberations concerned with the feasibility of holding a funeral may last as long as one week, during which time the corpse remains unburied in its hut. If the family council finally decides in favor of a *bunged*, a hole 5 feet deep is dug in the cattle corral of the deceased's homestead. A black ox is sacrificed and its skin will serve as a shroud for the deceased. The corpse is drawn up in a sitting

Elders at a beer-drink, seated in front of a hut.

position, its shroud slit so that the head protrudes through the opening. After the head is anointed with butter by the sons and wives, the body is placed in a sitting position (facing east) in the hole and the earth that was removed is replaced in the opposite order of its removal. A vigilance is set up over the grave by neighborhood young men delegated to protect the grave from being dug up by predatory hyena. Young vigilantes are permitted to eat the meat of the sacrificed ox that is near the grave. Quiet joking is heard as the young men roast small pieces of beef over a fire nearby.

During the first month of a funeral a mound (made of mud, cow dung, and poles, 4 feet high) is built over the grave. Over an eight- or nine-month period, three different layers will be added to the original monument, resulting in a cone-shaped mound approximately 12 feet high, 8 feet thick at the base, and 3 feet wide at the top. With each construction of a layer, a larger congregation of clan and lineage members assembles to assist in building the monument and brewing the honey-beer or *ghamung*, which is consumed as an essential part of the magico-religious complex surrounding the funeral. Responsibility for brewing honey-beer during the entire funeral ceremony is increasingly extended from the immediate family to the lineage and finally, in the eighth month, to the maximal lineages that segment the clan. Another round of brewing is organized among the maximal lineages and drinks are offered to the deceased through a special hole in the side of the funerary monument. At this time, the allocation of brewing quotas to various maximal lineages and major lineages is determined according to seniority and juniority as well as by reference to the maximal lineage of the deceased. Sometimes, quarrels over assigned brewing quotas lead to conflict and permanent fission between major lineages of a maximal lineage, when dissatisfaction arises over restrictions on beer consumption. The largest beer quota is assigned to the maximal lineage of the deceased.

The ritual and political head of a clan, *ashohoda dosht*, presides over a clan council hearing complaints that arise during the course of a *bunged*. He has legal power to impose sanctions against any adult clan member who does not attend the funeral of a clansman, or who arrives late and his absence affects the correct performance of a particular ritual. Sanctions against errant clansmen range from ridicule to cattle fines, depending upon the severity of the offense.

Fighting between clan members during the course of a *bunged* is an offense so serious as to be outside the jurisdiction of the clan head and is dealt with on the tribal rather than clan level. A tribal moot, *girgwaged getabarak* or "council of the wide tree," is convened by a spokesman, *ghamata girgwaged* or "mother of the council," and elders from different clans are summoned to the district to participate in the legal proceedings. The tribal moot is not convened until after the funeral ceremony has been completed. The protagonists remain to stand trial and the entire proceedings are presided over by a judge, *dinagochand*, a representative of the tribal chief, or by the tribal chief himself. The tribal chief is then referred to as Dinagid, the name of a mythical hero-jurist revered for his impeccable judgment in intricate matters requiring a kind of Solomon-like decision.

Lesser disturbances that do not result in blood-letting are either handled by individual spectators or else are corrected by the intervention of family or lineage members. Social control during a *bunged* is made difficult by the large quantities of honey-beer that must be ritually consumed. Indeed, a funeral is remembered by the number of participants and the number of beer pots brewed by all.

On the final day of the eight- or nine-month funeral, a black ox is brought to the gate of the kraal and is coaxed to enter. His behavior is watched closely for it is believed that any hesitation or reluctance of the ox to pass through the gate is a sign of disapproval of the deceased clansman's personal character. The ox should be willing to give up his life for the deceased. Once inside the kraal, the ox is tossed to the ground near the monument and suffocated. A leather thong is wrapped around his face clamping the jaws shut and his nostrils are stopped up with cupped hands until he no longer breathes. When he is declared dead, the men's group dance around the sacrificed ox and the monument and then retire to resume their beer-drinking. An elderly woman is selected to skin and carve up the carcass, sending the fatty hump to the clan head who is entitled to this portion. She keeps the ox-skin, which is now considered to possess magico-religious properties because the sacrificed animal had contact with the supernatural.

In the afternoon of the final day, women gather near the monument to sing religious songs to God and their ancestral spirits. Young men are assigned tasks of carrying water, firewood, and filling in the top of the monument, while young girls dance outside the kraal with some of the young men who have managed to elude the work assignments of their elders. As the sun nears the western horizon, a group of singing men carry a litter supporting a large grass sod and circle around the kraal. This grass sod, *guhelik* or "curls," has been guarded from the day that it was decided to give the deceased a funeral, and no cattle were allowed to graze near the grass located by a lake. The *guhelik* is symbolic of the deceased's hair and will be brought up by ladders to the top of the monument and placed in position. Before the *guhelik* can be brought into the kraal, a secret opening must be uncovered in the side of the thorn-bush fence to permit entry of the group carrying the grass sod. For guarding and opening the secret gate, *bisird*, the husband of the deceased's eldest daughter will receive one cow from the deceased's heir as payment for services.

When the grass sod is carried to the top of the monument, the first son of the first wife climbs up and, pushing a long branch into the top, recites a prayer to God. Then, rather than eulogize his father, he begins a speech of self-praise, telling the spectators about all of the times he helped his father. At the end of the speech, the son waits until the first son of the second wife offers him a cow to entice him to climb down. Ascending the monument, the first son of the second wife tells the audience that a *bunged* is a custom that should be preserved forever. Every eldest son of every wife of the deceased climbs up to place a tree branch in the top. The last person to climb up is the father or brother of the deceased's last wife. He places the deceased's herding stick and sandals on top without speaking. It is now getting dark and people begin to vacate the cattle corral and enter the huts or go outside to await the final ritual. Two very old men are selected to crawl naked to the deserted cattle corral and funerary monument. While tying a magic vine around the base of the monument, they whisper to the deceased, "Don't hurry. Wait for us. We will join you soon." It is now dark and the people await the return of the two elders before they can leave the huts or resume their dancing, singing, and drinking.

Immortality is believed to be conveyed to the man buried under the monument. After a few rainy seasons, the earthen mound falls apart, but some of the poles begin to sprout and grow into a cluster of trees. This then becomes a sacred grove to which survivors of the deceased and his clansmen make pilgrimages to appease his spirit and solicit his aid.

Only exceptional women are honored by a ritual burial. These are women who have borne many children who are now married and have children. A woman's *bunged* is a simple ritual compared to the funeral of a man, which is a clan affair. Her brothers, sisters, sons, and daughters, organize the rituals that last only a few days. The burial of the corpse is similar to that of a man, with the exception that no ox sacrifice is made and only a small monument of mud, cow-dung, and poles is erected over her grave. A small quantity of honey-beer is brewed for her brothers and sons. Her clay cooking pot and spoon are placed upside down on top of the monument and, in the closing ritual, the first wife of her first son sticks a cleaning rod through the overturned pot, saying, "Take your

Young men filling in the top of a funerary monument in preparation for the closing ritual honoring their deceased clansman. He lies buried in a hole beneath the monument.

The morning after the final funerary rite. Sandals and stick of the deceased are atop the monument and a magic vine is in place around the base.

pot and your spoon." Putting a hole in the pot symbolizes to all that the work
of the deceased woman on earth is finished.

Dissolution of a Family and Its Herd

Death of a wife in a polygynous household does not lead to the break-up
of a family, whereas the death of a husband signals the end of a household and
family and the division of the family herd. A leviratic union may prevent the
dissolution of family and cattle herd, but if this choice of preserving the original
marriage and family is not exercised, then the end of the *bunged* signals the
end of the polygynous family and its family herd.

On the day following a funeral, or an exposal to hyena, a circle of thorn-
bushes is constructed around a solitary tree and the family herd placed inside.
Then, the late husband's favorite bull is tossed to the ground and suffocated,
thus making "widows" of the cows in the family herd. Skinning the bull, *giild*,
"to circumcise," must be performed by a circumcision specialist from the Bisiyed
clan or by an alien tribesman who may be residing in a local trading settlement.
For his services, the "circumcisor" receives the hide and all the meat he can
carry away with him. The rest of the carcass is left for the hyena with the exception of a small portion of chest meat that is tied to the end of a stick and
used to touch the rumps of the cows as they file out of the thorn-bush enclosure.

Each wife then takes off her outer leather skirt and throws it to the
ground, saying, "Hyena, eat this." She also breaks one of her clay cooking pots.
The heir of the deceased takes his father's spear and breaks it, but the iron blade
is kept. Having performed these simple gestures of breaking with the past, the
wives and their children then face the task of separating the family herd into
their respective stock holdings. They may choose to continue residing in the
homestead for a few days or weeks, but it is only a matter of time before each
hut-group will go its separate way, back to the wife's father or to a new neighborhood. They continue to offer beer, tobacco, or milk to the deceased through a
hole in the side of the funerary monument, as long as they reside within the
kraal or in the neighborhood. As the grazing requirements of the cattle become
more difficult to satisfy, the building of a new homestead will take the family
members farther and farther away from the grave of the deceased and the
propitiation of his spirit will be discontinued. They will remember or be reminded of their neglect of the dead when misfortune again strikes their homestead.

9

The Changing Scene

Livestock Marketing Scheme

THROUGHOUT most of the German and British administrations, the Barabaig lived in social and cultural isolation from the rest of East Africa. With the absence of a European settler population, the process of urbanization and acculturation that affected other traditional areas in East Africa did not reach the Barabaig. Of course, some cultural innovations were introduced into Barabaig culture and society, but these new ideas and material goods were either easily absorbed or adjusted to by the Barabaig people. Livestock marketing was one of these new ideas and as long as participation in the scheme was left on an individual voluntary basis the idea did not seriously affect the traditional cattle-complex. Sale of cattle was merely another pattern added to the cattle-complex, until the government attempted to change the Barabaig from seminomadic pastoralists into stock raisers.

In an attempt to involve the Barabaig in the national economy of Tanganyika, the British administration devised a livestock marketing scheme that would operate in conjunction with a program of veterinarian services. The introduction of veterinarian medicine would reduce the incidence of disease in Barabaig livestock and the surplus stock would then be sold at local cattle auctions. Initial impetus to sell stock would be provided by the imposition of poll tax and cattle-head tax, to be paid in cash. Any failure to pay taxes would result in a jail sentence (hard labor). Faced with the problem of paying taxes in cash or going to jail, Barabaig cattle-owners chose to sell some of their animals. Unlike men from horticultural tribes who had to migrate to urban areas and work as wage laborers in order to raise enough money to pay taxes, the Barabaig were able to realize enough money from the sale of cattle to allow them to remain in their traditional area. From the sale of one bull or barren cow a Barabaig cattle-owner could pay his taxes, court fines, and other assessments and still have enough remaining to buy cheap trade goods at the local trading settlement. Seminomadic pastoralism discourages the accumulation of material goods and the Barabaig did not buy any consumer goods that required the expenditure of a large sum of money. Their material needs were few and easily met by the few trade items on the half-filled shelves of the local shops run by Arabs, Somalis, and Indians.

Since there are only a limited number of purposes for which a Baraband can use money, he views the sale of cattle as a European idea that has only limited utility and purpose for him. One of the remarks often heard around a cattle auction is to the effect that money cannot reproduce itself like cattle. Some Barabaig men remark that it is more pleasing to look at cattle than to look at money. Because cattle figure so prominently in the very fabric of Barabaig life and give it meaning, the sale of cattle is seen as a kind of necessary evil that should not be repeated too often. As Barabaig have observed, money disappears quickly but cattle are always there to see, hear, touch, and to sing to. The possibility of depleting a herd through frequent sale is recognized by most herd-owners, although a few men may improvidently sell stock for beer money. They will be reminded of their foolishness at the next ritual gathering of relatives or clansmen.

Barabaig view cattle as a kind of investment which, environmental conditions and "luck" permitting, will continue to increase over the years. A single cow in her lifetime may bear ten calves who, in turn, may each produce ten offspring, and so forth. Therefore, most of the animals destined for the cattle auction are either decrepit bulls who can no longer walk to pasture or barren cows—animals that are no longer economic or social assets according to Barabaig standards. Cattle are a form of conspicuous wealth and wealth is measured in terms of the size of a cattle herd and not in the accumulation of alien currency.

Introduction of government-run veterinarian services into Barabaig territory was initially viewed with suspicion when a number of inoculated cattle died because of poorly refrigerated vaccines. After overcoming the initial distrust of cattle inoculation, more Barabaig herd-owners brought their animals to be inoculated against a wide variety of cattle diseases and allowed their herds to be sent through chemical dips to rid them of ticks and other cattle parasites. Reduction in livestock deaths soon led to an increase in the size of cattle herds resulting in serious overgrazing and soil erosion problems. The government officials had hoped that the cattle market would "siphon" off the surplus cattle that normally would have been killed off by disease. They had not taken into consideration the strongly entrenched cattle-complex of the Barabaig. With an increase in numbers of cattle, the Barabaig had greater opportunities to use these animals in traditional ways—to obtain another wife, to make stock loans to clients—and, therefore, resorted to the sale of cattle at a local market only for immediate money needs.

To counter the Barabaig tendency to accumulate large cattle herds, the government of Tanganyika imposed a culling program that would force the Barabaig to sell more animals. Culling, or stock reduction, has been no more successful as a solution to cattle over-population than was the idea of cattle markets. Failure to specify the sex of the animal to be culled resulted in a program that could not attain its objectives. Owners of large herds, forced to sell some of their stock, chose old bulls and barren cows, and while there was a temporary drop in the cattle population the numbers of cattle again rose to their former levels. Had it been specified that only female animals were to be culled, a more efficient check on cattle population growth could have been achieved. The government was then reluctant to put pressure to sell more stock on the increasingly hostile Barabaig for fear of open revolt. Thus, the solution of one problem created other problems with possibly more serious consequences. Faced with the prospect of continuing an unimpressive cattle market, government officials asked themselves and others, "How can we get the Barabaig to sell more animals?" For them, the answer lay somewhere within the cattle-complex.

An End to Cattle Raid

One of the traditional solutions to the problem of increasing or rebuilding a cattle herd has been the institution of the cattle raid. Young men from poor families organize raiding parties and lead them into neighboring tribal areas where horticulturalists keep some livestock. The Gorowa and WaNyaturu tribes have been the hardest hit by these raids and occasionally a number of herdsmen have been killed in defense of their cattle.

Recouping stock losses due to famine or disease has been accomplished through the cattle raid. Of course, loss of livestock may be corrected by going to relatives and begging them for additional stock. But, if their herds have been similarly decimated by famine or disease, they are usually reluctant to part with any of their animals. Therefore, the cattle raid serves as a possible alternative to solicitation of stock from relatives. However, it is an alternative which is not without an element of danger. Members of Barabaig raiding parties have been killed and wounded by the arrows and spears of defending alien herdsmen.

Raiding neighboring tribes for cattle has long been a Barabaig custom that has periodically incurred the wrath of government officials. In response to threats of self-help retaliation by neighboring tribesmen, government forces have been sent into border areas to prevent large-scale intertribal warfare. One such incident occurred in 1955 at a place called Mtinku, in WaNyaturu territory.

A large group of WaNyaturu men, armed with bows and arrows, massed for a retaliatory attack against the Barabaig who had been carrying out numerous cattle raids against WaNyaturu cattle-owners. The WaNyaturu sent a message to certain British officials informing them of their plans. A truck convoy carrying police was rushed into the area to prevent an armed confrontation between WaNyaturu and Barabaig. Accompanied by a police force, several WaNyaturu elders entered Barabaig territory to search for their stolen cattle. Since it was the dry season, the task of locating stolen livestock was not difficult. They waited near the crater lakes for the Barabaig herds to arrive and picked out cattle bearing WaNyaturu brands. Some Barabaig men were arrested for possessing stolen livestock but the problem of cattle theft had reached a point where it became necessary for the Tanganyikan government to apply more stringent measures.

At a meeting of British officials and WaNyaturu elders, it was decided that a heavy cattle fine be imposed upon the entire Barabaig tribe, making them collectively responsible for their repeated practice of cattle-raiding. A fine of 500 head of cattle was levied against the Barabaig, said fine to be paid in cash to the WaNyaturu as compensation for stock losses suffered as a result of Barabaig raids. Using government tax records as a guide, each Barabaig clan was assessed a cattle fine, figured in terms of the size of its membership and their ability to pay the fine in cattle. Eight of the largest clans were each fined 20 head of cattle for a total of 160 head; the remaining 53 clans were fined cattle ranging from 17 head each down to one animal each, paid by the smallest clans in Barabaig society.

When the time came to sell the animals at the cattle auction, the Barabaig clans brought in their poorest quality stock. Knowing that the Barabaig would have to sell their stock to pay the government fine, and seeing the poor quality livestock, the Somali cattle-buyers, representatives of different meat packing companies, bid very low on the livestock brought to the auction. The sale of compensation cattle netted the WaNyaturu less money than had been anticipated and the Barabaig again proved their ability to find solutions to minimize their stock losses.

An End to Ritual Murder

Every human society experiences changes in its cultural repertory, either as a result of environmental changes, innovations by societal members, or as a consequence of ideas and actions of aliens who use peaceful persuasion and example or threats and applied physical force to achieve what they believe to be necessary and desirable change. The Barabaig have not been spared from various outside pressures, peaceful and hostile, to change their ways.

With the defeat of the Germans during World War I the area known as German East Africa came under the British mandate as the Tanganyika Territory. For more than forty years, Barabaig ritual murder of neighboring alien tribesmen continued despite numerous hangings of convicted murderers. Wide publicity was given to these hangings in order to convince the Barabaig that the hangings indeed were taking place, but these executions had little deterring effect on the institution of ritual murder.

Christian missionary activity among the Barabaig had little impact on their traditional value and action systems. Most missionary activity occurred along the northern borders with the Iraqw horticulturalists. On March 6, 1958, a Protestant mission was established deep in Barabaig territory. For ten years, the task of converting Barabaig to Christianity was a slow process with few converts and little effect on traditional Barabaig customs. Then, almost overnight, a dramatic series of events changed the situation and its repercussions are still being felt today. In March 1968, an African mission teacher pedalling his bicycle near his home in WaIsanzu territory was speared and mutilated—a victim of Barabaig "ritual murder." Government armed forces were quickly brought into Barabaig territory and physical force was drastically applied. Spears and sticks were confiscated and burned. Hundreds of Barabaig young men were rounded up and pressed into National Service both as punishment and reeducation. The independent government of Tanzania succeeded in doing what the German and British governments failed to accomplish; it brought large numbers of young Barabaig in direct face-to-face confrontation with the social and physical world beyond their tribal borders. It will prove to be an experience that will accelerate social and cultural change among the Barabaig for years to come.

Vanishing Cattle-Herders

Human societies have been herding domesticated animals for about as long a period of time as societies have held the discovery of plant domestication. Over thousands of years, the ranks of the cattle-herders have steadily diminished while the numbers of horticulturalists have increased in those areas and times not yet affected by the Industrial Revolution. In many parts of the world the transition from cattle-herder to garden-cultivator was made voluntarily and without notice by the rest of the world. At present, the number of cattle-herding societies is decreasing, and it will only be a matter of time before the Barabaig of Tanzania will be among the missing.

The independent government of Tanzania has decided the cultural fate of the Barabaig. It has banned the wearing of traditional clothing and is seeking to force the Barabaig to settle down in a permanent location, to give up cattle-herding, and to practice garden cultivation. All of these changes and more will eventually destroy the traditional life-ways the Barabaig have created over the centuries. Another island of cultural diversity will have disappeared into oblivion.

Glossary

BARABAND: Singular of Barabaig.

BRIDEWEALTH: The transfer of valued property from the family of the bridegroom to the family of the bride.

CLAN: A social grouping composed of living (and dead) members who claim common descent from the founder of the grouping but who cannot actually trace all of the links to the founder.

Dosht: A Barabaig clan, also the name for gate.

ECOLOGY: The study of Man's cultural adjustment to the organic and inorganic elements of his environment.

HEIFER: A young cow that has not given birth to a calf.

KRAAL: An enclosure or stockade around homes.

LEVIRATE: A continuation of a marriage in which wives of a deceased husband go to live with the late husband's brother.

LINEAGE: A subdivision of a clan. A social grouping composed of living (and dead) members all of whom can actually trace each connecting link up to the founder of the group.

MOOT: A temporary, or ad hoc, gathering of elders with legal authority to sit in judgment and impose punitive sanctions against a person.

Muhaled: Barabaig cattle corral made of thorn-bushes formed into a circle.

POLYGYNY: Plural marriage involving a husband and two or more wives.

Samod: A living space or courtyard containing Barabaig huts.

SORORATE: A continuation of a marriage in which an unmarried sister of a deceased wife serves as her replacement or surrogate.

TRANSHUMANCE: Seasonal movement of people and animals in response to climatic and vegetational changes.

Recommended Reading

East African Cattle-Herding Societies

DYSON-HUDSON, N., 1962, Factors Inhibiting Change in an African Pastoral Society: The Karimojong of Northeast Uganda *Transactions*, N.Y. Academy of Sciences Ser.II Vol. 24:771–801.
An excellent account of Karimojong resistance to social and cultural changes proposed by Uganda Government.

———, 1966, *Karimojong Politics*. Oxford: Clarendon Press.
Detailed analysis of Karimojong political organization, with emphasis on ecology and age systems.

EVANS-PRITCHARD, E. E., 1940, *The Nuer*. Oxford: Clarendon Press.
A classic study of the Nuer, an Eastern Sudanic people with segmentary lineage system of political organization.

GULLIVER, P., 1955, *The Family Herds*. London: Routledge & Kegan Paul.
A good comparative analysis of two pastoral tribes, the Jie and Turkana of Uganda and Kenya, respectively. House-property complex and stock associates are emphasized.

HERSKOVITS, M., 1926, The Cattle Complex in East Africa. *American Anthropologist*, 28:230–72, 361–80, 494–528, 633–64.
Earliest descriptive summary of the cattle complex in East Africa.

HUNTINGFORD, G. W. B., 1950, *Nandi Work and Culture*. London: H. M. S. O.
A good account of Nandi economic organization with a brief history of culture change.

———, 1953, *The Nandi of Kenya*. London: Routledge & Kegan Paul.
A detailed account of Nandi political organization with analysis of age-sets and war organization.

KLIMA, G., 1965, *Kinship, Property, and Jural Relations among the Barabaig*. Ann Arbor, Mich.: University Microfilms.
A detailed study of livestock transactions and their social and political significance among the Barabaig.

MERKER, M., 1910, *Die Masai*. Berlin: Dietrich Reimer.
A descriptive study, in German, of Masai material culture with some folklore and grammar.

SCHNEIDER, H., 1957, The Subsistence Role of Cattle Among the Pakot and in East Africa. *American Anthropologist*, 59:278–300.
A good summary of exchange and consumption utilization of cattle among the Pakot of Kenya.

SPENCER, P., 1965, *The Samburu: A Study of Gerontocracy in a Nomadic Tribe*. Berkeley and Los Angeles. University of California Press.
An excellent and detailed study of the Samburu of Kenya with emphasis placed on social problems related to age-set political organization.